The **SHARK** Technique
for Rapid
Re-Employment

By

Larry Arrance

This book is a work of non-fiction. Names and places have been changed to protect the privacy of all individuals. The events and situations are true.

ISBN: 1-4107-8938-1 (e-book)
ISBN: 1-4107-8937-3 (Paperback)

This book is printed on acid free paper.

1stBooks – rev. 08/30/03

The **SHARK** Technique for Rapid Re-employment

Are you a passive Bottom Feeder in the world of job seekers or do you aggressively hunt for the most desirable positions available? If you had to describe your method for finding great job opportunities, how would you describe it? Are you like the countless number of unemployed or underemployed who gather in large groups, most often unwittingly, and chase after the few jobs that are tossed out by companies that were forced to resort to advertising the position?

Life led you to where you're today, holding this book. Whether you buy this book or skim through it and put it back, will tell me which you're, a Bottom Feeder or a Shark.

What were the circumstances? Did technology change your world or were you downsized, restructured, adjusted, or any number of euphemisms used to soften the blow of your lost job? Don't waste another minute of precious time or another unit of much needed energy rehashing about what got you to this place. You're here. Deal with it.

Now before you get offended, I think that you show definite signs of having SHARK potential. A real Bottom Feeder would never have had the nerve or inclination to pick up this book. Before you begin to pat yourself on the back too vigorously, I have to take this opportunity to tell you that it was your Bottom Feeder habits that created your current woes. If you had always utilized the SHARK Techniques you wouldn't be reading a book on finding another job.

Okay, that's the last time I'm going to give you any more grief about past mistakes, unless you force me. As a Shark, you're going to be in greater control over your employment situation. You will be the one to decide how long you stay and when you move on. As a Shark, you will glide through the waters of the work world with greater confidence and presence. The Bottom Feeders will be watching you pass them by and wonder why you're so lucky at landing the choice positions. They will attribute it to luck but you and I will know that it was your SHARK Techniques that gave you the edge.

What is the SHARK technique for Rapid Re-employment?

Sell yourself through every step until they offer you the job. Do your **Homework**. Know the company you're going after. Identify the problem that you're going to solve for them. Create **Allies** for your campaign. Recruit people to help you in your cause who can also look for opportunities for you. **Repeat** every step until you succeed. This is a game of numbers. Obviously, the more times you put your offer in front of a buyer the greater the chance someone will buy. **Knowledge** about your product is absolutely critical. No sales manager would dream of sending out a sales representative without them having learned a great deal about the product.

How should you use this book? If you want the best results, develop your knowledge and skills starting at the beginning. It's like the old saying "Don't just learn the tricks of the trade, learn the trade." Looking for work is a skill you can use for the rest of your life, so wisdom would suggest that you acquire a good grasp of the basics. If you learn the SHARK Technique thoroughly, you may never need to experience unemployment again.

Sometimes a person's circumstances demand that you take the first job opportunity that presents itself. If your situation urges you to go to the specific chapters related to what you need right now, then go for it but come back and utilize the entire book when you get the chance. I want you to develop the SHARK Technique so that you never find yourself in this position again.

A good way to distinguish how a Bottom Feeder and a Shark read a book is to look at what they have in their hands. The Bottom Feeder will be holding the book and possibly a beverage or even the remote to the TV. A Shark will be holding the book and have a pen and highlighter handy to make notes or mark out information that is vital to their needs. A Shark knows that learning isn't a passive activity. They know that learning a skill takes more work than merely reading about it. So if you haven't got your pen and highlighter handy, go get it now!

Table of Contents

1. What's Inside the Package? 1

2. Do What Madison Avenue Does. 13

3. How far is too far? 25

4. Warning, This for Adults Only! 39

5. Why You Shouldn't Go Fishing with a Victoria's Secret Model. 47

6. There is No "I" in Team but There is in You're Fired. 59

7. A Dynamite Document or a Liner for a Birdcage? 71

8. You'll Make Them Smile When You've Got the Right Style. 91

9. Cover Me I'm Going In! 101

10. Taking it from a Letter to a Lethal Weapon. .. 111

11. What Do They Really Want? Cracking the Want Ad Riddle. 121

12. Recruiting Your Army. 127

13. Thirty Seconds and You're In! 143

14. Discover Where Most of the Jobs are Hiding. 155

15. Utilize the Ultimate Weapon for Getting Past Barriers. 167

16. Surf's Up! 177

17. They're Free and They Work! 189

18. "We Have Ways of Making You Talk." 199

19. Be as SEXY as You Can and Make Your Answers PAY. 213

20. Okay It's My Turn. 229

21. Where Bottom Feeders Kill Themselves. 237

22. Hiring a Professional Hunter 245

23. Rinse and Repeat... 251

Congratulations, you just demonstrated Shark-like behavior. A bottom feeder never would have read this far. They're still out there waiting for a job to come floating down from above and land in front of their face. A Shark like you knows that a job worth having requires keen senses to recognize an opportunity and the developed hunting skills to seize it.

Why should you read this book and not one of the other job search books on the shelf? Because this book was written for real people - not just executives who haul home hefty six-figure salaries. Sure, an executive could utilize the advice in this book, and it would help him snare an even better position but I want everyone to have that opportunity. Many of the books I've read on this subject sound like a fresh batch of blah, blah, and blahs.

Shark techniques are different. The techniques are simple, aggressive and effective. Simple, - because anyone can use them. Aggressive - because it puts you on the offensive. Effective - because you will land a new position faster than you thought.

Chapter 1. What's Inside the Package?

Sales managers would never dream of sending a sales representative into the field without making sure they had acquired the basics on Product knowledge and customer benefits. What do interviewers complain about the most? It is the interviewee's inability to communicate what they can do for the company. Their inability to explain the skills and abilities that would make them suitable for the position can leave the interviewer guessing. Before you can ever make a sale, you have to match your benefits with the needs of the employer. And before you can tell them about your benefits, you have to know what they are.

It's about now that a bottom feeder begins to turn pale and starts to stutter. Because they have never really thought about what benefits they bring to the workplace, they don't know how to tell anyone about them. You won't make that mistake. You need to have a clear idea of what you can do and what you could potentially do. Will it take some time to learn about what you have to offer an employer? Yes, but not nearly as long as you might think. It is this investment in yourself that will pay huge dividends as you cash in on bigger and better employment opportunities.

When you have a good grip on your strengths, weaknesses, and preferences, this will have an immense impact on choice of career, how you handle yourself in an interview and your continued success in the workplace.

Transferable skills are ambiguous words that have been bandied about for some time now. Unfortunately, very few job seekers know what these words mean. The dictionary tells us that transferable is something that can be taken from one place to another. It is mobile.

Transferable skills are a higher rated than your core skills or natural talents. They're also highly marketable because they're needed for a wide variety of jobs and can be transferred from one task, job or workplace to another. The more transferable skills you can offer an employer, the easier it is for them to see you as the best candidate for the position. I met a Shark that told me before she goes after a position she researches it to make sure there will be new transferable skills she can acquire. She knows that, in order for her to remain marketable, she has to constantly expand her base of transferable skills. Brian Tracy in "Accelerated Learning Techniques" said it best. "What you know today, won't guarantee you success tomorrow." Transferable skills are skills you'll need to develop to continue to land the right jobs during your work life.

When it comes to describing your transferable skills, they come in three definite categories. They are adaptive, technical and interpersonal. Adaptive skills revolve around your capacity to adapt to new situations, people and working conditions. Can you adapt to the needs of the moment? I have met individuals who are so rigid and inflexible that when a change of any size occurs, it throws them for a loop. You can spot the difference between how a Bottom Feeder deals with change and how a Shark deals with it. The Bottom Feeders immediately panic and concern themselves with how the change is going to affect their lives. They stress out over what they might lose. A shark demonstrates a positive attitude towards change. For a Shark, change is synonymous with challenge and more often than not, creates an opportunity. The first thing a Shark asks themselves when a change is on the horizon is "Why is this a good thing? How will I benefit from it and what are the opportunities here?" If you were an employer, who would you want helping your company through the fastest changing business environment in all history?

Technical skills are your so-called hard skills. They include your ability to communicate in the written form whether that means creating and drafting documents, sending memos the traditional way as well as electronically. Gathering information through research and being able to relate that information to others. Sorry, but you won't impress too many employers with your ability to "surf the net" or download jpegs and music files unless it is somehow relevant to the position. And when you do collect the data, do you know what to do with it? Do you have the ability to process it, analyze it, utilize it and store it? Can you operate a computer? For many of the bottom feeders, when someone talks about the "C" word, it is worse than Cancer. I met a woman who had

3

worked for a large employer for fourteen years. The company was changing many of its functions over to a computerized model. When they offered to send her for training on the computers, she panicked. Her solution to the problem was to quit!

If you're in the position where you still have not acquired the ability to operate the dreaded computer, stop right now and make a note to yourself to take the next course available. This isn't a luxury skill any longer. I was told of an occupation that used to require a simple clipboard and pen but now has hand-held computer devices. Other positions that traditionally employed people with a grade ten or less education, now routinely asks for at least a grade twelve graduation because there will be computer in use. In the book "Mega Trends" they refer to people who didn't bother to keep up with technology as "Techno Peasants." Unfortunately, these people will have to fight amongst themselves for the ever-dwindling number of lower paid – lower skilled jobs. Not a place a Shark would ever find himself.

Basically, technical skills covers any skills that utilize your analytical abilities, mathematical abilities, organizational skills, capacity to speak more than one language, including speaking the language of computers. Are you proficient in the use of software? For some occupations, you only have to know the basics because you may be using an in-house program. For others, getting around inside a word processor will be sufficient and for others you may have to know programming or building web pages. Don't panic if you tend to be a technophobe. Your key transferable skills could revolve around your ability in public presentation or your artistic abilities. Can you draw, draft, paint, or even play an instrument? Technical skills even encompass your spatial and mechanical skills. In other words, can you visualize something you're working on or can you operate a piece of equipment and possibly repair it? In the simplest of terms, a technical skill is something you can physically demonstrate for the employer.

Ever heard the phrase "I'm a people person"? I'm sure you have and I hope it's something you can say about yourself. Why? Unless you have high aspirations of becoming a lighthouse keeper or lone assassin, you're going to be interacting with other people. Of the people who get fired from positions, over 90% lose their jobs because of inability to function on a social level, not because they couldn't do the job. Why do you think businesses are encouraged to replace workers with robots or to source the work out to contractors? The vast majority of headaches for management come in the form of employees. Equipment doesn't get into fights with other pieces of equipment. It won't sabotage other equipment's work in order to climb the corporate ladder.

They have a saying in the work world. "Hire slow, fire fast." From an employer's point of view, the employees are walking time bombs. They could say or do something at any moment that could blow up in the employer's face and possibly cost him his company. Let's imagine that you're the employer and I work for you along with several women. Being the loving and supportive guy that I'm, I offer encouragement to my fellow coworker in the form of a friendly pat on the behind. Who does she sue? You guessed it! You get sued. I get the thrill; you get the bill. Doesn't seem fair, does it? This is why it is so critical that an employer finds people with well-developed interpersonal and social skills.

A socially adept employee will know how to listen effectively, communicate clearly and use tact and diplomacy. They will work well with a wide variety of people regardless of age, gender, social or economic background, choice of religion, political beliefs, physical disability or special needs. Someone with effective social skills is capable of helping others solve problems and can develop strong and healthy working relationships.
These people will add value to the workplace by coaching, or mentoring or assisting others to become better at their jobs. They won't be focused only on their own little world.

People with good interpersonal skills tend to lead by example. They can be good leaders or good followers. Employers can depend on these people to inspire trust and respect from their coworkers. I met one of the exceptional "People Persons." She worked at a branch plant of a national company. In a typical, underhanded attempt that some larger companies use to reduce costs, they fired her after seventeen years of service. They sent in their axe man from head office to do the dirty deed. As cowards do, they waited until the end of the day and asked her to stay a little late. All the other 89 employees had left the premises. They told her she was finished and told her to clean out her desk and leave.

It took about thirty minutes for the news that she had been let go to circulate through the plant. 87 employees left their jobs and went to her home to comfort and support her. They had come to love and respect this woman because she had always treated them with love and respect. The workers were men and women, many of them young enough to be her children. Her interpersonal skills had allowed her to create such a strong working relationship with her coworkers that they were willing to risk losing their jobs to support her. She had what a lot of smart employers call *customer service skills*.

You might be thinking that your job never brings you into contact with any customers. Get rid of that thought now! Everybody we deal with is a customer. There are outside customers and inside customers. Outside customers are the people who buy our products, use our services, write our paychecks. The inside customers are our coworkers. To give good customer service to our coworkers, we need to do everything within our power to make their jobs run as smooth as possible. When you do that the whole company runs better and you stand a much greater chance to receive your just rewards.

Passion in the workplace? Is that even possible? Yes, and I'm not referring to an affair with a coworker or sleeping your way to the top. I'm talking about discovering what you want to do on the job that will make you want to be at work.

I discovered my niche almost by accident. I say *almost* because at some level I believe there are no accidents and everything happens for a reason. My life went through a series of what seemed like cataclysmic changes and I found myself unemployed and attending a government sponsored training program. It was there that I was exposed to what would become a passion for me - facilitating classes for adults. Now, the changing careers didn't come without expenses. When I made the change from my previous career to facilitating, I now earned about one third of what I used to take home but I was three times happier. Work was no longer work. It had become a pleasure. There were even times when my weekends were irritants because they kept me away from what I loved doing.

Before you race out and become a facilitator of classes and workshops understand that it isn't any specific job or occupation that creates this unheard of kind of bliss. I talked with a dentist who told me that he looks forward to coming into his practice on Mondays because he loves what he does. A meat cutter told me that he enjoys what he does so much that the day just melts away and before he knows it, it is time to go home.

Identifying what motivates you, what gets your juices flowing is key to knowing what intrinsic needs you have that have to be fulfilled in order for you to experience true job satisfaction. For me it was things like the constant learning of new skills, making a difference in people's lives and meeting lots of interesting people. For you it could be creating something new and exciting, building something that adds value or beauty to someone's life or being recognized for making a contribution. Whatever your needs are, and remember they are your needs and not someone else's, it is important that they get met.

I have had people tell me that their main motivator is money and lots of it. I feel sorry for these people because if acquiring money is their main goal, they are never going to be happy. When you chase money you find out there is never enough of it. How many millionaires long to be billionaires? Should money be one of your motivators? I think so. Unless you have figured out a way of living for free. For those of you who have gone home to live with your parents, just try and convince me there isn't a price for doing that.

There is a simple system for identifying what your intrinsic needs are. Take out a piece of paper and draw a circle in the middle. Sticking out from the circle are ten spokes or lines. In the center of the circle write the name of the occupation or career that you're considering. On each of the lines write down what you will get from it.

Let's imagine that I've placed the occupation of accountant in the center of my circle. Being an accountant would give me 1) money 2) fame 3) groupies. Okay, I guess it's pretty clear I don't know much about what being an accountant is about. By the way, that's about all I could think of in the way of reasons for me to be an accountant. Is being an accountant a good occupation? Absolutely, but not for me. When I did this exercise using the occupation of writer or facilitator, I can fill all ten spokes. When you do this exercise, the key is being able to fill in as many lines as possible with what you will get from it. Anything over eight lines is a good indicator of a good career for you. Anything under five was probably somebody else's suggestion and should raise some real concerns as to whether it is a smart choice for you. Have some fun with the exercise. Keep trying different careers until you find three that has lots of rewards for you.

I'm often asked: "'How do you know when you have found your niche, your ideal occupation? For me, was when the thought of retirement held zero appeal. When you love what you do, why would you want to escape from it forever? When I hear people counting off the days, months or even worse years before they can stop working, I'm saddened. I think to myself, "Why are they wasting their lives doing something they hate. What if they never make it to the magic year when they can pack it all in? Did they waste a life?" None of us are given a written guarantee that we will make it to retirement. Find your niche and enjoy your work because you never know when you will be taken out of the game of life.

Bridges are used to get you across an expanse that stands between where you're and where you want to be. You need to know the length of the bridge and whether you have the commitment to get to the other side. Discovering all that lies between you and your goal is called doing a Gap Analysis. Let's imagine you want to be a Civil Engineer. We would place the words Civil Engineer on the right side of a blank piece of paper. On the left side of the paper, we write where you're right now. Let's say you're a high school dropout with a couple of credits needed to complete your secondary education. You also have six years experience in the construction industry. Bridging this gap will mean completing the steps necessary to get from lack of education to holding a degree in Civil Engineering. It is crucial that you build your bridge with tiny, doable steps. Many a bottom feeder would look at that gap and proclaim it was a bridge too far.

When I say the steps have to be doable, I mean it. No one said that going after your niche was a weekend project. If you want it bad enough, it will be worth the journey. When I was making my transition from the logging industry to that of being a facilitator of adult workshops, I worked during the day at a job I didn't like while I worked for free in the evening delivering classes. I invested time and energy into developing my skills until I could find a paying position for my facilitating. Does it matter that your journey takes six months or six years, as long as you get to where you're doing what you love? Contrary to the saying "it's the journey that's important", getting there is all that matters.

If you don't have the necessary education, go and get it. If you don't have the needed skills, go develop them. Remember, it is referred to as carving out a niche. Not having a niche fall into your lap! You already know that where you are is not good enough or you would never have purchased this book.

Chapter 2. Do What Madison Avenue Does.

Special offer, special deal, or special delivery are words that we see emblazoned on products everywhere. Why would advertisers go to that effort to make their product seem special to us? Because we've been raised to respond to the word "special". A few examples are *special occasion*, that *special someone* or in that *special place and time*.

Before I send clients out to apply for a position, I encourage them to come up with five key reasons why their product is special and stands out from the rest. Why would an employer pick them over the other hundred or more applicants? It is <u>your</u> five key reasons as to why you're special that will have them offering <u>you</u> the position.

I will ask my class "If you were an employer, would you hire you?" The general response is a resounding YES! On occasion, I will get someone who says, "No way, I've worked with me before and I don't like the effort I put in." After that outburst of information the rest of the class a pretty good idea as to why that person is unemployed. If your answer was yes, then why, why would you hire you? Is it because of your work ethic, your training, your dedication, initiative, drive, history of success or your outstanding attitude? Whatever the reasons are, it is your job to convey that to the employer. If you're like many of the Bottom Feeders and have trouble selling or promoting yourself, I have three words for you: GET OVER IT! If you don't sell yourself, who will?

I'm not saying that you should be as blusterous as the genie in those Bugs Bunny cartoons who, whenever he burst from his lamp, would start proclaiming "Let the banners fly and the bells ring out, I'm here. It's too good to be true but I'm here!" But you will have to sell me on something because if you don't, the person behind you in line will and they'll walk away with the position. Better to err on the side of overconfidence than shyness. Would you buy a product the seller was reluctant to say anything good about? Remember, the job may not go to the best qualified, or best person for the job but it will go to the person who did the best job of selling themselves.

Problems arise in every job and in every industry. What did you do to prove you were the solution to those problems? I can tell the last job title of every person that walks into my classroom before I speak to them. They were problem solvers until they no longer offered a solution to a particular problem and that is why they were let go. And I know what their next job title is going to be. They will be a problem solver again. When you come at a job search from that angle, it makes the task very easy. Study a company. Discover what their problems are, determine how you can solve that problem and convey that you're the solution. Bingo, you have a job! Bottom Feeders miss this point every time because they are so focused on their own problems.

Keep this next point firmly in mind and you won't have a problem marketing yourself. "You can't sell if you don't match benefits with needs." It will not matter one bit what you have in the way of benefits if they don't address my problems or needs."

They say that people buy only two things: solutions to problems and good feelings. In order for you to get an interview, your resume has to be a solution to one of the employer's problems. The good feelings will come at the interview when they believe you're the best solution to their problem.

Because being a great problem solver is such a strong selling point, it is important that you know how to convey that you're that kind of employee. To do that, I recommend that you use the STAR format to demonstrate your skill. **S**ituation; **T**asks, **A**ction and **R**esults.

Describe a situation or problem that you or your company faced. Describe the tasks or steps you believed would be necessary to bring about a happy conclusion. Describe action steps you actually took. Finally, inform the interviewer of the results.

Example: A client came in at the end of the day, all in a panic because they had just been called in for a job interview for first thing the next morning and had been told to bring an updated resume with them. We were just closing so there wasn't time to do the new resume. The client was very upset. The task was to find a way to produce the new resume before the client's interview without getting staff to stay beyond their normal working hours. My action was to take down the appropriate information from the client and complete the new resume at home that evening on my own time. The result was a very happy and grateful client that went to the interview with confidence.

Take the time to go back through your jobs and come up with as many examples as you can. This will accomplish two things. It will give you great ammunition to use in an interview and it will solidify in your mind that you're a great problem solver.

Saving money, generating cash flow (creating an atmosphere where the employer can do those two things) are all the employer is interested in. They will not hire you because their bank accounts are swollen and about to burst and they need a way to get rid of the money. Before you try to market yourself to the employer, you need to get focused on their *Greed Gland*. Business is about profit. Pure and simple. Even non-profit organizations have to keep costs down and funds flowing in, to stay alive. So how are you going to do that for them?

Will what you have to offer make their life easier, richer or more productive? If you weren't a solution to some of their concerns, then why would they want to talk to you? When I'm coaching a client on how to approach a company or business, I will ask them to consider what the concerns may be for the manager or owner, for that position. Is it generating sales? Is it expanding the client base? Is it keeping costs down by eliminating waste? Or is it creating a strong team that can do all three? Communicate to them how you're going to do any or all of those things and the position is yours.

Bottom Feeders spend most of their work life trying not to be noticed and end up never accomplishing anything worth noticing. If you have been guilty of this, make a vow to be a stand-out employee in your next position.

Quick learners are worth their weight in gold. One of the biggest costs of bringing on a new hire into a company is training. There is always a cost. Maybe you have the formal education and experience for the position but there will be certain things that are specific for this position. That means it will take at least a minimal amount of time to train you to their way of doing things. The price tag depends on how long it takes to get you to the point where the employer is making money off of you all the time. You had better be able to demonstrate to the employer that you adapt to new working environments and procedures in minimal time.

This shouldn't be too difficult. I once took an accelerated learning course and the first thing they had me do was to take out a blank sheet of paper and start writing down all the things that I had already learned. How long do you think that would take? A very long time, which was their point. I was already a learner and had proven it many times. Their goal was to make me a much better learner. So think back, what are some of the skills, techniques or procedures you have learned during your life? Pick out some of the better ones. Choose examples that are related somehow to the position you're pursuing.

Your ability to describe in tangible ways that you're a quick learner will put the employer's mind at ease about whether or not you will be able to pick up the new skills necessary to become successful in this position. This leads me to my next point. Are you what the industry calls a Lifelong Learner? Bottom Feeders are content to stick with what they already know. There is a maxim that grows truer every day in the Information Age. "What you know today won't guarantee you success tomorrow." Sharks are always looking for an edge. They firmly believe in the adage "the more you learn the more you earn."

Courses are offered year round from night school programs, correspondence or over the Internet. A Shark will have study goals set for each upcoming year. They are constantly researching to see what skills or abilities will make them more marketable. Considering that the average full time job lasts between two and three years, the odds are pretty good that your next job will not be your last. Knowing this, it doesn't make sense to stick to the same set of skills or knowledge base and expect to be continually employed or employable. Only a Bottom Feeder would live under the illusion that the next job won't require additional skills. Considering that many of the jobs that will be coming their way will be attached to new technologies or ways of doing business, to not seek new skills is to condemn themselves to obsolescence.

Bottom Feeders are short-term thinkers. They focus on getting through the workweek. An energetic Bottom Feeder might go so far as to plan their activities for the up-coming weekend but that is all. Sharks have some idea of where they will be one, two and even five years down the road. Knowing this keeps them focused on which skills they need to develop or upgrade. It also keeps them aware of what direction a company is headed. This knowledge will allow them to determine how if they are going to grow with the company.

Many the people who come to my classes don't get it. They still approach the training concept from the wrong perspective. Brian Tracey uses this example to motivate people to seek out training opportunities. Let's imagine that you enroll in a course. The course is 100 hours in length. You apply yourself with determination and you walk away with a skill that earns you $10 per hour more than you were making before. You have a full time job. That means you work about 2000 hours in a year. So you will have earned $ 20,000 extra from that new skill. A skill can be expected to last about 3 years before it needs to be upgraded or replaced. That means you earned about $60,000 from that new skill. If we go back to the original 100 hours that you invested in acquiring that new skill, it figures that you were being paid $600 per hour to take the course. From that point of view, was it worth your time? Let's be more conservative. We'll say that you earned an extra $5 per hour more. That means you were being paid $300 an hour to pick up a book, sit in a class or pay attention. Was it worth your time? Bottom Feeders consider going back to school or attending training courses to be drudgery or an inconvenience. Sharks see training as an investment in their future earning potential.

Don't do what most Bottom Feeders will do. They wait for someone to provide the training for them. If a company will provide training of any kind, jump all over it. If they don't, seek it out yourself. Remember this is your career, your product, and your future. It is your responsibility to make sure that your skills are up to date and ready to market. I had a client lament over and over about how unfair he had been treated by his former employer. He had had a very good job with the Federal Government. His complaint was that they let him go after his seven years of service with them because he wasn't bilingual. He thought they had done him wrong because they knew how important it was that he be able to speak both official languages of Canada. They had never, during his seven years in their employment with them, bothered to send him to a course so that he could acquire the second language. Like a true Bottom Feeder, he wouldn't take any responsibility for the situation. He knew how important it was to have the second language yet didn't bother for the seven years to take the initiative to learn to speak the language. If you know that a skill is critical to your success at your job, why are you leaving the responsibility for acquiring it in someone else's hands?

Some of you're going to do a pretty good impression of a Bottom Feeder and whine about the cost of acquiring new skills and training. A Shark can acquire the new skills using methods that are often free and only require effort on their part. There is a place in your city that dispenses free knowledge. It is called the Library. It's filled from floor to ceiling with information just begging to be read and absorbed. When was the last time you visited the library and took out a book that could increase your value in the marketplace?

Another thing that has always amazed me about Bottom Feeders is that when one of them breaks from the rest of the group and signs up for a course, they figure they have done enough and sit back and wait for the course to begin. It could take several months before the start date and they don't prepare for the training at all. Along comes day one and they pick up their books, find out what lies ahead and stumble their way through. A Shark would have researched what the course entails, went to the library and started doing some reading ahead of time, so that when the course began they would already be in high gear and have the jump on the other students.

Seeking to make yourself more valuable to your employer is the key to staying employed. A typical Bottom Feeder approach to employment is to do only what is asked or is expected. A Shark will focus on looking for opportunities to draw attention to their contributions to the success of the company. I met a very career aware woman who made a point of journaling what she did on the job. She would create an opportunity every three or four months to present the information to her supervisor. The result was she received three wage increases to everyone else's one. She was smart enough to not do what most Bottom Feeders would do: put their careers in the hands of their supervisor. Guess what? Their supervisor already has a full time job of taking care of their own career. How much time and energy do you think they will commit to cultivating the careers of the staff below them?

A Shark looks for opportunities to volunteer for new assignments that will enhance both their image in the company or industry and develop new marketable skills. Don't sit back and wait until a boss or supervisor to approach you with a project or assignment. Take the initiative to ask where you can help or what direction the company is going. An even better career move is to adopt an *intrapreneurial attitude*. Much like an entrepreneur who creates businesses an intrapreneur creates business for the company for which he works. If you want to shine for your company and make yourself an asset that they can't do without, become an intrapreneur. Stay vigilant. Keep your eyes and ears open to avenues that would bring new streams of income to the company. Most Bottom Feeders in an organization are looked upon as liabilities and not assets. That is why it always looks so appealing to upper management to reduce costs by getting rid of employees. If you're an ongoing source of revenue and growth for the company, you guarantee your employability.

New and innovative are words that make an employer start to drool because they speak directly to the greed gland. As a society, we are hooked on "New", "Fresh", "Cutting Edge". How many people do you know that go around asking, "So, what's old?" That's right; it's always "So, what's new?" Every company that wants to stay competitive needs to be growing and expanding. This doesn't mean they have to become larger in size but it does mean they have to flex with changes in demands of the economy and technology. Edward Demming, the man who played an instrumental role in creating the Japanese Business Model, promoted the policy of Kaizen, which refers to the process of constant improvement.

Bottom Feeders are content to do what they've always done. This limited way of thinking is suicide in the employment world. There is a saying that is forever dragged out at MLM meetings. "Do what you have always done and you will always get what you have always got!" Many people lived by that rule for too long and now they paying the price. MLMers use it in the proper context. It is to get you to try a different approach so that you will experience different results. Bottom Feeders make the mistake of believing that if they just put their heads down and continue with their same old, same old they'll continue to enjoy their steady stream of paychecks and benefits. What

23

happens when your same old, same old won't fit the needs of today's marketplace? It is called unemployment. A Shark will adjust to the times and ride the wave to the future instead of being crushed by it.

Chapter 3. How far is too far?

Limits are not restrictions. They are there to guide us. Knowing the limits to what you will and won't do for your job is very important. Some people refer to our limits as values. Identifying what you value can determine if an occupation or career is right for you. Maintaining your integrity will allow you to look at yourself in the mirror without contempt. If you take on tasks that go against your values, the only result will be disaster.

I know, for myself, there are occupations and jobs that would wreak havoc on my value system. Occupations that require me to exploit people's weaknesses like alcohol, drugs or gambling wouldn't work for me. Nor could I work in an industry that put people's lives in danger like manufacturing guns or munitions. Other people may not share my view of those industries. That's okay. All of our values are just that - our values. Do I pay a cost for sticking to my values? Yes! I know of people who are making immense amounts of money owning a chain of wine and beer outlets. Sure I could make a lot of money but it would never pay for the damage to my integrity.

So determine where your boundaries lie on what you will do or won't do. The limits you set now will save your health, sanity, relationships, and maybe your life someday.

Excelling in a career often means that the person is utilizing their natural talents and skills. Victor Frankl, the founder of Logo Therapy said that there are four categories of work.

H/H	E/H
H/E	E/E

H/H stands for Hard / Hard. This refers to work where the necessary skills were hard for you to attain or learn. No matter how long you do them, you never ever find them easy. For some people, their hard/hard is using the computer. They can be shown the basics a thousand times and it just won't stick. For each of us it will be different. But the one thing we can say for certain, it isn't a good choice for a career.

E/H stands for skills that were easy to learn but the work never gets easy. An example of this would be digging a ditch. It wouldn't take long to teach you how to dig a ditch but it is a job that never becomes easy. Same for chopping wood, it doesn't take long to learn but it is always going to be a chore.

H/E stands for skills that were hard to learn in the beginning but with sufficient practice you can do it pretty much without thinking. If you ever learned how to type, you might remember practicing for many hours until your fingers seem to breeze across the keyboard without hesitation. For many of us there ceases to be any real challenge and little personal satisfaction with keyboarding all day.

E/E refers to skills you have that you can't quite remember when or where you picked them up. They seem to be skills that other people have difficulty acquiring. These are your natural talents. When you find your niche, they will certainly be a major part of it. So think about the things that you're good at and, in all likelihood, they will be things you enjoy doing. There is a reason you were given those talents or skills. I heard one psychologist attribute many of the problems that plague our society today stem from too many people not expressing themselves through the use of their natural talents. Their belief is: frustration is the result of stifled potential.

Now I'm not saying that if you don't find your niche you will end up in dire consequences or even prison. But for many people, it may feel like a prison.

Reality bites and it doesn't care how nice you're, how smart you're or how much you deserve to reach your goals. There was a time in my career as an employment coach when I would have my class do an exercise that would give them some ideas on what careers they were best suited to according to their likes and dislikes. The process was halted because more often than not it did more harm than good. According to the computer-generated results, they would be told that they could be Marine Biologists, Nuclear Physicists, or Publishers. For some of these people, this created a fantasy world for them to hide in. It also created an immense barrier for me to overcome to convince them to seek out more mundane jobs that were more suited their current skill and educational levels. A good many of my clients had never completed high school, didn't have two dimes to rub together and had families to support. Dangling a dream occupation in front of them like a gold plated carrot was just plain mean.

For some clients, making goals that were too far beyond their reach was just what they wanted. It seemed that because a computer told them this is what they could be doing, anything else was beneath them. And if what they were meant to do was out of reach, then they should continue to do nothing. Now, you might be thinking that those goals were attainable if the person really wanted them. I agree. But the brutal reality of their situation meant that the sacrifice on their part was going to be immense. So stop and take a look at your goals. Are they doable? Are they reachable or are you setting yourself up for failure? Should you pick something far below what you want or are capable of doing? Of course not but it might make more sense to set a series of goals with each getting you one step closer. This way you get to experience several successes instead of the possibility of running into one huge failure.

For a person that wanted to become a Marine Biologist, I would have suggested he find a job related to the industry and work during the day and finish his high school in the evening. This is doable and it would give him a chance to see if he even liked the industry.

Support for your job search or career change is vital. You will find that there may be support systems already in place around you. These can come in the form of your friends, family and government sponsored agencies or organizations. Tap into all of them. It doesn't make you look weak by asking for help. And no, it doesn't make you more heroic to tackle it all on your own.

Government agencies can support you by providing advice on local labor market trends, job postings and career search tactics. Many of them may be set up to help you with the costs of doing an effective job search by covering things like photocopying and faxing costs. I'm going to let you in on a little secret. Squeaky wheel gets the grease. I often found that many government sponsored agencies would bend the rules or try harder to meet the demands of someone who was persistent and unwilling to take no for an answer. How many times do you think they helped these people out just to get rid of them?

Your friends can help by keeping their eyes and ears open for job openings and keeping your spirits up. Your family can provide emotional, motivational and, in many cases, financial support. The average length of time that someone is unemployed is nineteen weeks. You will find that it takes a lot less when you have help. So take it. Could you do this entirely on your own? Probably, but I think it would be a safe bet that the journey would be harder and lonelier. Don't let your pride extend the length of time before your next job offer.

Clarity is power. One of my mentors would hammer that into my head. That statement carries so much truth to it. Knowing where you're going makes everything easier. How successful would you be at planning your travel route if you didn't know the destination? Do you have a plan? There isn't much point making a great deal of effort or taking giant steps forward if you don't know where you're going. Before you can break your journey down into steps, you need to know the final destination. I'm always amazed when I ask a client what kind of work they are looking for and they reply with "I don't know" or "oh I'll take anything." How will you know a good opportunity when you haven't a clue what it might look like?

You say you have a plan. Is it written down? Have you broken it down into doable tasks? When you do this, you'll see which tasks can be done right away and which ones will take longer. It makes much more sense to take baby steps in the right direction than to take several gigantic steps away from your goal. Remember that *Clarity is Power*! There's a simple exercise I do with my class that you can do with the help of a friend. Have your friend hold an ordinary sheet of writing paper between their hands. You stand in front of them and place the palm of your hand flat against the paper. Have them keep the paper taut and you push in with your full weight. The paper will support you. Now, I want you to do the same thing again, only this time use your outstretched index finger and press into the paper. It will burst. This visual demonstration shows that the impact is always greater when the energy or effort it is focused instead of being spread out. So, make a plan for either your job search or career plan. Oh, and by the way, did I mention that *Clarity is Power*?

Barriers may pop up from time to time. I believe they were placed in your path to test your commitment to your goal. When I was just making my career change, I was facing some major barriers. My relationship at the time was on shaky ground because I think my significant other had run out of patience with my career transition. Finances were in the toilet, I was just getting by on my unemployment benefits and I didn't have any clear idea of when my facilitating career would take off for sure. I had been putting in massive amounts of time and energy and had only seen a trickle of income flow back. There was pressure to abandon my goal and return to my previous career. The pressure became immense when an opportunity was offered that paid three hundred dollars a day to return to my old way of life.

I wavered for a moment but my perseverance kicked in. The thought of going backwards after all my hard work was unthinkable. My decision to ignore the golden carrot was rewarded with a job offer to facilitate classes on a full time basis about 6 weeks later. You should expect that these little tests could be thrown onto your path. Don't let anyone or anything dissuade you from doing what you must. If you cave in at the first sign of resistance, you will regret it for the rest of your life. History is full of sad stories about people who stopped on the edge of success when only a few more steps could have changed their lives forever. Don't become one of those sad stories.

Any opposition to capturing that great new job or beginning your new career will make the completion of your journey that much sweeter. If you think about an obstacle course, those obstacles were meant to be challenged and defeated. Any obstacle can be climbed over, stepped around, dug under, or blasted through. A Shark doesn't understand the meaning of *no*.

Bosses, or to be more specific, bad bosses are the biggest catalyst to people choosing self-employment. I'm going to let you in on some news. You have been self-employed all your life and always will be. When you go to work, whom do you go to work for? You, that's who. This is great news because you get to enjoy the power and autonomy that comes with being self-employed.

This makes you the president of *You Incorporated*. This means that you're in charge of the training and development department, the marketing department and the billing department. When you begin to see yourself as a bundle of services that can be marketed to any number of customers, instead of someone's employee, you will feel an immense amount of power and freedom. If you're employed as you're reading this book, then think of your employer as your best customer for the time being. They have not always been your customer and they won't always be your customer. If you're looking for work right now, you're looking for the best bidder for your services.

By being president, you have to make sure that your training and development department is making your product more desirable and valuable. As head of the marketing department, you need to keep your promotional material up-to-date and attractive to customers. You should make sure that the marketing department is busy letting your customers know how valuable your services are. Your billing department needs to establish what your services are worth and convey that to your customers.

Self-employed people are much more proactive and understand there is a direct relationship between taking action and reaping rewards. By considering yourself self-employed, you will stay outside the trap of just looking for a job. Remember, your main focus is to find someone to pay you for your services. This can come in the form of temp, contract or piecework. Don't let the labels trip you up. What difference does it make as long as you're getting paid?

Fear can be crippling. It can stand in the way of taking the required steps. Some of you're focused on finding security. You're hooked on the idea of landing a union job. I'm not saying that you won't but the number of union jobs is decreasing at an alarming rate. Douglas McArthur said, "There is no security, only opportunity!" He was right. How many people do you know who worked in unions and had their security blankets torn out from under them? Their security blanket became more like a shroud. With many companies outsourcing the work and many an employee going to work everyday with their blinders on, they left their employment and careers in the hands of the company. If you were guilty of that mistake, take this opportunity to regain control of your career.

Remember, the greater the challenge, the greater the reward. I can remember the first time facilitated my first few workshops. I literally got down on my knees and prayed that no one would show up so I wouldn't have to get up in front of people. Lucky for me, and my career, the prayer was ignored. I had to pass through the fear to discover the most rewarding experience of my working career. When you break through your fear, you will discover the same thing I did. There is nothing on the other side of the fear.

When I look back at my fear of having to stand in front of strangers and lead a workshop, I have to laugh. Those first two nights were a lot of fun and I created some great friendships. It's like the author Susan Jeffers said, "Feel the fear and do it anyway."

Making a successful career change of any magnitude or going after a plumb job will depend, to a large extent, on your belief system. Have you ever completed any major undertaking? Do you have a history of being successful? I'm going to bet that you do, even if you don't believe it right now. It is critical that you believe in the likelihood of your journey coming to a successful completion.

There's an exercise that we do in class that begins with my asking the class "How many of you would like to make a lot more money? How many of you would like to be in much better physical condition?" As you would expect, many hands go up. I then tell them that whatever is in their bank account or whatever shape their body is in, are just results. The same holds true for the jobs you find or the condition of your career.

I will then ask them "What determines the results that we get?" The answer is actions or behaviors. The things we do on a consistent basis will give us our results. Next, "What determines our actions?" Thoughts precede our actions. Look around the room that you're in right now. Everything in the room began as a thought first. What we think will determine what actions we will take.

"What determines the direction our thoughts will take?" Our belief system is the guiding force. There is a direct link between our belief system and the results we experience in our lives. You will not rise higher than your personal belief system will allow. It took me quite awhile to separate myself from my past career because I kept seeing myself as just an ex-logger. I would tell myself that others wouldn't hire me because I was just an ex-logger. The result of that belief system was that I wouldn't apply to most jobs because I thought it would be a waste of time. For almost three years I went from laboring job to laboring job. My prospects for ever having a rewarding and challenging career seemed very bleak. Luck smiled on me and I was laid off from an another low paying laboring position. I did what most Bottom Feeders would do and went to the nearest government-sponsored office that specialized in helping unemployed people.

I joined the other Bottom Feeders in going through the job postings looking for a job with my name on it. A large poster on the wall caught my attention. It announced a Work Based Placed Training program for unemployed people. There were several enticing components to the training program that could ultimately improve my work situation. The Shark in me told me to take the chance. Good fortune was with me and I was one of sixteen chosen from the large number of applicants to take part in the program.

It was during the twelve weeks of in-class training that I had the opportunity to watch two facilitators in action. I was enthralled. They were so skilled at facilitating that it looked incredibly easy to do. When I found out that their backgrounds hadn't always been teaching and were similar to mine in many ways, the belief that I could be a facilitator was firmly planted.

I then did something very Shark-like; I approached one of the facilitators and asked what I needed to become one of them. He informed me that there wasn't an actual school for facilitators unless you were connected to some large organization. Being very supportive, he recommended that I find someplace that would let me instruct and the keep them informed of my progress. Most Bottom Feeders would see this as a catch 22 situation and give up. The Shark in me decided to go for it. I knew what I needed to do. In order for me to instruct classes I would need a few things: first a classroom, then some students and finally a curriculum.

The something to instruct was the easiest. I was drawn towards the Self-esteem exercises because of how much better they made me feel and the obvious impact they had on the other participants. I wanted to share this experience with more people. My next step was to decide to whom I was going to instruct a self-esteem class. The first group that came to mind was the native population in our area. I knew from experience that many had low self-esteem and could benefit from the classes. So I contacted a drop in center that the First Nations operated. I suggested that I could facilitate classes in the evenings for free if they could provide a room. They were very excited about the offer and said they would do the advertising for me for free.

My decision to make this career change was given a big thumbs up. As it turned out, I had some natural talents in the field of facilitating groups because on the second night of the classes one of the participants asked me how long I had been leading classes. I told her that this was the second class. She responded with "I know it the second night but how long have you been doing this?" When I clarified to her that this was only my second time ever, she was very surprised, she thought I had been doing it for years! I attributed the success I experienced to the brilliant role models my facilitators had been for me.

The classes ran on a weekly basis for about six months. The irony was that during that time, I only had one native fellow come to my classes and only because he ended up in the room by accident. All my classes were comprised of the general public. As I was becoming more of a Shark, I made several trips to the offices of my mentors to keep them apprised of my progress as a facilitator. I knew whom I wanted to work for and so I let them know of my goal. My opportunity came when they offered me a short six-day contract to facilitate self-esteem classes for a group of single mothers.

The classes proved so successful that a couple of months later when a full time position instructing classes opened up, they came to me first. Being a Shark paid off. The rest of this book will focus on honing your SHARK hunting skills so that you can enjoy the sweet taste of success in the job market.

Chapter 4. Warning, This Chapter for Adults Only!

Taking initiative is a Shark attribute. Employers don't want to baby-sit their employees. Employers expect you to strive to be productive at all times. A young woman I had the privilege of working with told me her answer to the question "Sometimes the workload can be light, what do you do with your time?" Her answer was "I clean. I like to keep busy. So if there isn't anything for me to do, then you will find me organizing and cleaning my work area." That is the sign of a Shark. Myself, whenever the demands for time were light, I would take the opportunity to do research on topics related to my job.

Lack of initiative was the sole reason that one of our clients wasn't kept on as an employee. As I mentioned earlier, we had a training program where our clients were matched up with employers who offer eight weeks of training for free without the obligation of hiring the participant. 85% of the employers kept the trainee after the eight weeks. I sent this man out to his training place host. After two days, I called the boss to see how the participant was working out. They informed me that the fellow was a good worker but as soon as there was nothing to do, that's what he was doing. Once his assignment was completed, he would sit in a chair until someone came along with another task. What would this guy do if no one had come by for a long stretch of time? Would he just sit there collecting dust? The employer gave him a few more days to impress them but his behavior remained the same. They terminated the relationship at the end of the week.

This guy didn't get it. Most Bottom Feeders don't. This was an opportunity to make an employer sit up and take notice that you're a good employee and they would be lucky to have you. What could the guy have done to impress the employer? He could have sought out someone to get more assignments, offered to help another employee or picked up a broom and started cleaning. A Shark will search for ways to be seen as indispensable. I worked in a machine shop during the day, while I facilitated workshops in the evening, until I could facilitate full time. I busted my butt making sure whenever my task was completed that I would resume cleaning up the shop. They told me later that they kept me around for nearly two months longer than the season normally called for because I made myself valuable on a full time basis. Sharks are not attracted to opportunities to be idle.

"People who don't take risks generally make about two big mistakes a year. People who do take risks generally make about two big mistakes a year." Peter F. Drucker Mistakes are a part of life. Employers know that you will make mistakes. Their concern isn't that you will make them. Their concern lies in your inability to admit them. You may remember an episode of "Mad About You" when Paul Riser made a mistake but was unable to admit it. The closest he

comes to admitting his mistake was when he said he "wasn't as right as he normally is." In the show, it's funny. In real life, we don't see the humor when the people we work with can't admit that they made a mistake. It is a sign of maturity when we hold ourselves accountable.

During a class on Interviewing Skills, I happen to ask one of the participants if he had ever had his driver's license revoked. Now, I don't have a clue about a participant's driving history so I never know what the answer will be. He admitted that he had lost it. By the time he got to end of the story it, was totally the officer's fault. What had he told me? Yeah, he wouldn't accept responsibility for his actions. I could be wrong but I doubt very much the police officer stopped him out of boredom, forced him to drink copious amounts of alcohol and then encouraged him to drive away so that he could stop him for impaired driving. Some people think that life is a series of lessons. If that was the case, this fellow would be repeating this lesson until he gets it.

You will make mistakes, unless, you plan never to do anything new ever again. What is important is that you learn from the mistake. An employer wants to know that your mistakes have made you a better, wiser, more valuable person. Some mistakes have turned out to be very fortuitous. It was said that Coca Cola was never intended to be a soft drink. The story goes that it was the result of a pharmacist named John Pemberton. John was cooking up medicinal syrup in a large brass kettle. He was trying to create an elixir or tonic to cure a number of ailments. His assistant added it to some ice water and discovered it was tasty. The second batch was made but included the accidental addition of carbonated water. The result was a fizzy beverage that is now sold around the world.

Other mistakes led to the invention of the chocolate chip cookie, Post-It Notes and Silly Putty. When you do make a mistake follow this advice: admit to it right away, take whatever steps necessary to make the best of the situation and identify what you learned from it. I've found that the longer you put off taking ownership of the mistake or try to hide it, the less forgiving the employer will be when they do find out. And don't kid yourself, they almost always find out. That being said, employers are not looking for someone who makes nothing but mistakes. Yes, there is an eraser on the pencil but, hopefully, the pencil wears out before the eraser.

Happy people make for a happy and profitable workplace. In order for people to feel happy, they need to feel accepted and respected. How tolerant are you of other people's differences? We live in an ever-changing sea of cultural, religious, political and lifestyle choices. Are you accepting and flexible enough that you can create strong working relationships with whomever your coworkers may be? When I was first hired as a facilitator, their main concern was if I was going to add to the strength of the team or subtract from it. If you have ever worked in any business or organization you know how much the dynamics of a workplace can change when they add a new person to the mix.

Good managers will strive to fill their staff with people who have well-developed interpersonal skills and an easygoing attitude. I have seen many companies comprised of loose knit clusters of cliques. Many of the cliques are cold and hostile to a new hire. Quite often, if the new hire is accepted into the clique, someone else is eased out to maintain some kind of balance. Much like children who take turns as to who isn't "in" until the alliances once change again.

Another problem that can plague a workplace is some people's need to be "right." My wife worked in a large business where their unwritten motto was "I would rather be right than happy." It was more important to some individuals to prove that they were right than to find a solution to a problem. Sometimes passive aggressive behavior would sabotage someone else's efforts. Instead of a team atmosphere where they all worked for the good of the company, which in the long run is good for everyone, it became an assortment of camps pitted against each other. As a result, the absenteeism was high and loss of key personnel to other less toxic businesses was a common occurrence.

High self-esteem and confidence are like two strong legs holding up a healthy and valuable employee. Do you like yourself? Do you know what your key strengths and abilities are? When I do exercises with my class that center around questions that reveal their self-image, you can feel the discomfort in the room.

Many are saddled with a mistaken belief that if you like yourself, then you must be conceited. That's a Bottom Feeder attitude. It is because of their low self-esteem and this attitude that they condemn themselves to live as Bottom Feeders.

A chief complaint of executives that hire people is that many applicants can't or won't express what their attributes are and reasons they should be hired over others. Some of you're going to tell me that you were raised not to toot your own horn or brag about yourself. I have some simple advice for you. BUILD A BRIDGE AND GET OVER IT! It is your job to sell me on why I should hire you. You'd better not be counting on your mother to come in behind you and tell them why you're special because you're too modest to say it yourself. You're expecting someone to pay you forty, fifty, sixty, ninety or over one hundred thousand dollars per year! You had better have some very good reasons for them to make that kind of investment because if you don't, the Shark behind you will. They will get the sale and you can swim back down to where the other modest, humble and toothless Bottom Feeders are waiting.

People with high self-esteem and confidence are a gold mine for an employer. They make better employees because they feel good about themselves and their abilities. This confidence means they are more inclined to take on new challenges and responsibilities. They tend to have better relationships at home and at work. People with high self-esteem are usually healthier and miss less work. For an employer it is win, win, win when they find someone with high self-esteem. There is an old saying "You had better learn to like yourself because you're taking yourself with you everywhere you go." How hard is it going to be to sell a product you don't like or believe in?

"Where will you be in five years? Do you have a plan for your life?" I'm always amazed when I ask my students this question and they just stare back dumbfounded. If I were to ask what their plans were for this weekend, they'd have an instant answer. When I have had the opportunity to meet them again, and again over the years (because Bottom Feeders tend to experience job loss many times), they are still no further ahead but they do have 250 weekends under their belts. Where are you going? What do you want to become? What would make your life have meaning? These are not pie in the sky, New Age questions designed to help you get in touch with your inner employee. These are valid questions. A Shark has a plan and every job or position is designed to lead them closer to their goal.

When I think back to when I was in high school, I had friends that knew what they wanted to be back in grade nine. What a difference that made because now every course or subject they took had been chosen with an end goal in mind. I didn't have a clue! As a result, I took courses that were of little value once I was out of school. Now, many years later, I look at their lives and at myself and it seems like they have accomplished so much more but in reality we are much the same. The only difference is everything they accomplished was in one direction while my achievements went in every direction. It can be compared to someone traveling on a journey. Each day they drive for 100 miles. The person with the plan to drive east would have traveled 1000 miles in ten days and find themselves in another province or state. The person who went out each day and drove 100 miles in a number of directions will still travel 1000 miles in ten days but isn't much farther ahead than where he started. Guess who is happier?

I not going to take up any room in this book to cover setting goals because I know if you're smart enough to have picked up this book then you probably have at least one book in your personal library that tells you how to set and achieve goals. Find it, dust it off and start planning your life. It's like the old adage "If you fail to plan, you're planning to fail."

Chapter 5. Why You Shouldn't Go Fishing with a Victoria's Secret Model.

The answer is pretty simple: because that's not what the fish are biting on.

What are employers looking for?

Major advertising firms always sit down and consider what the consumer needs and wants before they launch their campaigns. A Shark will take the same steps. How can you market yourself successfully if you don't know what an employer is looking for in an ideal employee?

My information is based on the results compiled by the Conference Board of Canada. Many major and high profile companies submitted what they considered were key skills, abilities and attributes necessary to be an excellent employee. To view the list of over 40 national and multi-national companies involved with the report visit http://www. conferenceboard. ca/nbec

Communication ranks at the very top. Written and oral skills, especially the language in which the business is conducted, are vital. Can you convey your message in the written form or by using a word processor? History is ripe with examples of how business has been lost or lives put in jeopardy because of unclear written communication. Can you describe a time when you have had to use clear, written communication? Did you have to send interdepartmental memos or submit reports? Did you have to create legal or sales documents? Did you ever write out instructions for a crew to follow?

Is your penmanship legible? I've worked with people who can't read their own chicken scratch, let alone have me read them. They will make the effort to leave a memo or message of varying degrees of importance only to find that no action will be taken on it. You cannot act or respond to a message that you can't read. I happened to be auditing a classroom presentation of one of my esteemed colleagues. She was a brilliant facilitator and was using an overhead as part of her presentation. It was necessary for her to use a marker and write her words on the overhead to make her point. I found myself trying to decipher the odd squiggles sprawling across the transparency. I looked out into the classroom and saw the puzzled looks on their faces. They couldn't make sense of the random assortment of wiggly lines. My associate looked up at the screen and said, "Oh my, I can't read anything that I've written." There was a collective sigh from the classroom when they realized it wasn't just them that couldn't read it. From that point on, she kept her writing to a minimum or took time to properly form each letter for ease of reading.

Can you use a word processor or typewriter? Now, you might be thinking that your job doesn't require the use of a word processor. I'm going to encourage you to change that mindset now. Just like several years ago when it became a basic benchmark to have your grade

12 diploma, the same now goes for having the ability to use a word processor. Because children in many primary and elementary schools are already comfortable producing their homework on the computer, it will be assumed that anyone can do it.

Reading and responding to emails isn't limited to forwarding the latest joke to your friends. Many employees are finding that their job requires that they be connected to the Internet. This means that there's a good chance that you will have access to email. Communicating through email can be a dicey situation. Because we can compose and transmit our messages before we've put a great deal of thought into them, there's the danger that we don't put enough effort to make sure our message is correct or clear. Have you ever had someone send you something and you weren't quite sure how to take it? Or have you ever sent someone a message and that person misunderstood your intent? The numbers of these types of incidences have risen so sharply that many employers have clamped down on interpersonal emailing among staff. Some employers have banned it outright. Remember, don't say something in an email to a coworker that you wouldn't say in front of the rest of the staff. After all, it is in writing!

As of the writing of this book, it's estimated that 30% of employees are connected to the Internet. Of that number, up to one third have their activities monitored by their employers. With some of the new devices, it is possible for employers to capture a record of every keystroke, every picture downloaded and even sites visited. So an intelligent employee will remember that they are at work and all their energies and activities should be work related.

Writing in the language in which you conduct business. I don't mean writing in English, French or Swahili. I'm talking about following recognized or accepted business etiquette and style. This is especially important if your job has you in any kind of administrative capacity. I know that I have struggled with this on many occasions. I like to think it's because I'm not anal enough to care about how many spaces go between the date and beginning of the contact person or business name and not my apathy on the subject. If you're interested or concerned with the proper layout for business communication then I recommend you get an updated book on business forms and documents. I recommend an updated book because it seems the people who decide what should go where, get together at a huge conference somewhere and vote on it. Talk about no life.

Reading a novel is different than reading a manual. Do you have the ability to read and comprehend technical information, graphs, charts and displays? Do you know how to extract information that is important to your needs? I remember working at a place where the employer walked up to me with a manual for a new computer program and told me to read it. That was my training. Fortunately, I was able to work through the manual and acquire the knowledge necessary for me to successfully utilize the program. If this is a skill in which you're weak, then I suggest that you ger out some of the product manuals you have lying around your home. Yes, you do have some and the chances are good that they have never been opened. Read through them a step at a time until you can make sense of them. If it doesn't come easily in the beginning, don't be discouraged. Technical reading is a skill that most of us don't learn in school but it can be learned.

Technology has always had an affect on people's jobs. This is nothing new. We can go right back to the invention of the wheel. The difference is that technological changes are happening at an ever-increasing rate and it takes a real effort to keep up to date. Basics today include knowing how to operate a computer. Computers have infiltrated almost every occupation. I know of jobs that were notoriously labor intensive that now routinely include the use of computers. Many pieces of heavy equipment from logging to milling now have computers attached to them. What was once done with a clipboard and a pen may now are replaced with hand-held computers. I spoke with a gentleman who goes around testing and monitoring equipment in the field. When he's done, he has to enter the data into a computer in his vehicle so that the information is instantly forwarded to a database.

If you're considering looking for occupations that don't require computers or the ability to operate computers, I caution you to think again. Remember the technopeasants I mentioned earlier? Theirs will not be a bright future. If you have not acquired even the basics, you had better put it on the top of your "to do" list. When I was a technopeasant, I knew that I wanted to acquire the knowledge and skills of the computer literate. But because I did not have the money to take a course, my first access to a computer came by way of a friend. This opened a door for me. I added to my knowledge base by volunteering for an organization. I did their grunt jobs in trade for time on their computer doing tutorials. Learning how to use a computer is essential to staying employable. Start today.

Common sense, unfortunately, isn't all that common. Employers are always on the lookout for people who can think critically and act logically. Can you recognize problems, analyze them and come up with solutions? Have you ever been around people who seem oblivious or, worse, apathetic about a problem that seems obvious to everyone else? Sometimes a policy or procedure may be in place in a work environment that doesn't help the business. Most Bottom Feeders would just blindly follow the directive regardless of the impact. A Shark would recognize that the rule is ineffective or even damaging and take steps to rectify the problem.

One of my co-workers has strong Shark tendencies. Whenever something comes up that would appear to be going against one of the company policies she asks herself "What would Ron do?" Ron by the way, is the employer. She asks herself this because she knows that Ron is a Shark and would take whatever action is necessary to bring about the best result. A Shark knows that a rule is rule only as long as it benefits everyone. Very few things in life are completely black or white. Do you have the common sense to look at the big picture and take actions that will produce the best results?

"You're the weakest link!" The only thing worse than having an incredibly annoying game show host announcing that to the television audience is to have that be the reason for being let go from your employment. The success of the business is often attributed to the health of team. Do you contribute to the health or are you more of a cancer that eats and erodes the group? Cooperation, support and synergy are the key ingredients of a happy, thriving and functioning team. I have worked in environments where you can feel the energy drain when certain staff members would enter the room. Many staff were uneasy when this person was present. They made a point of guarding or limiting their conversations out of fear that their words could and would be used against them at some later date. You know the kind of person I'm talking about. They live by the rule that if there are no rumors by ten o'clock then it's their job to start one. They thrive on chaos and dissension while none of the aftermath or fallout is ever their fault.

There was a man who worked in a large corporation and quite enjoyed his job for several years. A new manager took over his department. It wasn't long before the pleasure he had once derived from his position was all but gone. He decided that he couldn't live under the supervision of this man and contacted a head hunter firm to find him a new position. After thinking about it for a while, he realized that he didn't like that as a solution. He loved his job, the work that he did, and his fellow coworkers except for the manager. The Shark in him surfaced. He contacted the head hunter firm and had them find a position for his manager. They came up with a better job for his manager and he jumped at it. Sharks know that if you cannot remove yourself from the stressor than remove the stressor.

Speaking of managers…can you lead? Training others shows confidence, confidence in yourself to convey what you know in a way that others understand and confidence from your employer. Employers would obviously have to have enough confidence in the way that you do things for them to want you to train others to do it the same way. Not everyone can lead. We have all witnessed evidence of that. I have had the opportunity to see both good and bad leaders.

Respect is earned. Unfortunately, some people who have risen to upper levels of management or had it fall into their lap because of circumstances beyond their control or efforts. I know of one such person who had worked his way up to a position above his skills and abilities. His superior at the time was not ingratiating his way into the good books of the business owners because he had uncompromising principles and wasn't willing to be a "Yes" man.

When the owners realized that this man wasn't going to be manipulated, they replaced him with the next man on the totem pole. The effects on the morale of the company were noticeable within a couple of weeks. The management styles were completely opposite. The man with principles sought to encourage and motivate his staff through praise and support. The replacement manager lacked confidence because he knew he was in over his head. He decided he would rule with intimidation and an iron fist. He would belittle his sales team and tell them they were losers and leave it up to them to prove they weren't. The results were a demoralized staff that wanted to see him fail even if it meant their paychecks would suffer. It took less than a year with the new manager at the helm before the owners couldn't ignore the damage his style of management was creating. The manager found that his own iron fist crushed him.

Another gentlemen of questionable managerial intelligence had my services for one full week before I chose to leave for another job. He was so paranoid that his crew might not be working as hard as he thought they should that he parked his pickup where he could watch their every move. His crew became resentful of his lack of trust in their work ethic. I worked alongside these men and knew they were very hard workers. Some of them looked for ways to get back at him. Whenever an opportunity arose when they knew they were out of eyesight of the boss, they would purposely park their machines and do nothing. I asked one of them why they were just sitting there, he replied "if he's going to treat us like we're a bunch of lazy ***** (cleaned up bush talk), then we're going to make him pay."

To show you what a good boss looks like, I would have to hold up the two owners of Epicenter Resources, Inc. They lead by example. Their integrity was so unshakable that you trusted everything they did. I cannot think of employers who treat their employees better. They were such good judges of character that they instinctively knew what the potential of their employees were and handed out assignments accordingly. Opportunities for growth were given to those they believed would benefit from them and kept others where they were already flourishing. They never set up anyone for failure. The result of treating their employees with trust and respect was that many would often go above and beyond our normal job duties. Another indicator that their management style was effective was that turnover was minimal. The few people that did leave, left reluctantly. Each of them were lured away by such incredible career moves that were impossible to ignore.

Think about it. If you have managed or supervised before, how would you describe your management style? Would *you* want to work under *you*?

Sharks live by the motto "Lead, follow or get out of the way." A Shark doesn't mind being a follower if the person they are following knows what they are doing. But if you don't then don't waste their time. What kind of a follower are you? Do you take direction well? If an employer tells you what to do, can they count on you to complete the task in a timely manner or do you need to be monitored, supervised or cajoled into action? Sharks are looked upon as being good employees because they take pride in their work regardless of what the work is. They are dependable and can be relied upon to do the best job possible. A Shark sees every task as an opportunity.

A man I know owns several pubs and nightclubs. He told me the story of a seventeen year old that came to him asking for a job bussing tables. The man said he would give the lad a job but stipulating that he must work hard and remain drug and alcohol free. He warned the young man that should he ever come to work under the influence, he had eyes all over the place watching for him. The lad assured him that that would never be a problem because he really needed a job.

Nine years later, the young man invited his former employer and his family out to a pub. He told him that the meals and the drinks were on him that night. He told him that this was his way of saying thank you. Pointing to the room around them he said "If it were not for you taking me off the street and giving me a job, this place would never have become mine. I'm sure that if you hadn't taken me off the street, I would've been dead by now. You took me and taught me everything I know about this industry and that made it possible for me to own my own pub." Many a Bottom Feeder would not take a job bussing, washing dishes or serving customers because they'd think it was a dead end job or beneath them. A Shark looks at every job as a steppingstone. Quite often being a good follower can lead to a role in leadership.

Larry Arrance

Chapter 6. There is No "I" in Team but There is in You're Fired.

Dysfunctional doesn't just apply to the description of families. Many businesses suffer from dysfunctional relationships amongst employees. That's why many companies spend huge sums of money on training and seminars to help create healthy working relationships between staff members. A key concern for any employer will be how well you will fit into their *family*. Will you add to the synergy or will you cause strife and agitation? Remember 90% of those people that lost their jobs lost them because of poor social skills, not because they couldn't do the work.

One of the biggest complaints of employers who hire from business or tech schools is lack of interpersonal or communication skills of their graduates. Look at people who seem to shine in the workplace; they generally have well developed people skills.
How would you describe your capabilities in this area? Are you a good communicator? Are your interpersonal skills good enough that you can fit into an organization without disruption?

I hesitate to direct my students to any one particular service provider over another but in this case, I do make an exception. If there was one skill that you could develop that would be a boost to almost any career, it would be mastering the skill of communication. An excellent organization for developing all the facets of communication is Toastmasters International. I know there are other organizations dedicated to helping you become a good public speaker but this is the organization with which I'm most familiar. One of the key reasons acquiring this skill can be such a career booster is because, of the top ten fears in North America, speaking in public is number one. Learning to do this will help you leap frog past all those people who are crippled by the thought of speaking in front of others.

At the writing of this book, I have been an active member of a Toastmasters Club for about seven years. I have seen many members go through some very impressive career changes and growths. The key reasons for this happening is that as their ability to communicate develops and opens new doors for them ranging from training assignments, presentation and public relations to management. Think about what better communication skills could do for you. What career opportunities would open up for you?

Another benefit from developing communication skills is that you will experience less stress in the work force. There will be less stress because your odds of getting your message across clearly as well as understanding what another person is trying to say go up greatly. The Chinese have a saying "The first man to throw a punch is the one who lost the argument." Many troubles between coworkers or between staff and clients can be retraced back to a breakdown in communication. So the better you can communicate, the less likely you're to be on the outs with someone you work with. One of my clients, during the limited time we spent together, seemed to be a very likeable young man. While we were discussing the several, short duration jobs that he had held during his seven or eight years in the job market, it came to light that whenever he had a problem with another employee, he quit. He told me that the ideal job for him would be where there are no other people. I'm not aware of too many of those kinds of jobs out there other than perhaps lighthouse keeper or troll under a bridge. To make his dream job even more unlikely, he was striving to get into the hospitality industry. I guess no one had told him that the hospitality industry tends to cater to people.

My young client's dilemma leads me to my next topic - job expectations. Do you know what you want or expect from your job? I know that you expect to get paid for your work but what else does a job have to provide for you in order to get satisfaction? Most Bottom Feeders never consider this before accepting a position. That is why so many of them are miserable in their positions.

Satisfaction is something that you should and need to get from your work. You're going to be spending at least one third of your life working. Why would you set yourself up to spend such a major portion of your time here on earth doing something you dislike? Each of us will find satisfaction in different ways. For me, its knowing that I helped someone by showing them a better way to market their skills, give them hope and encouragement or make a difference in their lives. For others, it could be making life easier for others through creating high quality products, providing comfort and care, building things that will last, or knowing that you did a job well. If you take the time to determine what you want and need from a job, you're more likely to find a better position and avoid a miserable working experience.

Resilience and optimism will pay big dividends for an employer because it will determine how well you bounce back from setbacks. We've all heard many times that the only constant in life is change. Changes will come in any job and any industry. How well do you respond to it? Most Bottom Feeders are concerned about how the change will negatively affect their lives. What will they lose or have taken away? When there is a change in policy or procedures, or how you're expected to do business or maybe how a new manager wants the job done, do you fight it or try to make the best of it? Your answer will tell me what your resilience level is and how optimistic you're.

Being flexible means you can adapt to situations as needed. I've met many people who became rigid on the job and the results were never pleasant or profitable. Hopefully, you won't recognize yourself in my examples. Example 1: We used to offer a workplace based training program that connected potential employers with employees. I would find training opportunities for my unemployed clients. A company would agree to provide eight weeks of training to them in lieu of wages. The client would work for free because they could still collect their unemployment insurance benefits. The company was under no obligation to hire the client after the eight weeks but over 85% would because they now had a trained employee and they'd already seen the person in action.

I found a company that was willing to take on a client that had been unemployed for over two years. It took some extra effort on my part to make the connection because the company had a negative experience the year before when they'd tried to train someone on their own. After investing over $50,000 into this person's training, he showed his gratitude by accepting a job with another company once he was trained. The company would only accept him and the training program if we could expand the eight free weeks to twelve free weeks. As it turned out the unemployment insurance people wanted this guy back working very badly and were willing to make an exception in this case.

As a rule, I would check with an employer within two weeks of sending them a client to see how well he was fitting in but in this participant's case I waited a full month. The employer informed me that the fellow was learning fairly quickly and they liked his work. Their only complaint was that he seemed very rigid. The hours of operation were eight to five. They said you could set your watch by this fellow. By ten to five he was tidying his desk. By five to five he was putting on his hat and coat and was shutting down his computer. At exactly five o'clock his backside was seen going through the front door. The reason this bothered the management was that was not how they or the rest of the staff approached their jobs.

At this business, the work ethic was completing your task before you called it a day. That might mean working to fifteen after or heaven forbid twenty after. Before you start acting like a Bottom Feeder by saying that the company wasn't being fair by expecting people to work beyond the end of their allotted time, there is something you need to know about the company. They rewarded their people for their contributions and extra effort. They gave bonuses out at Christmas according to a person's contribution. This was 1994 and two of their employees were receiving bonuses of up to 20% of their yearly wages.

Their concern was that his habit of leaving his job at exactly five o'clock would become contagious. We agreed that they should call him in and let him know what they wanted changed about his performance. After explaining their concerns, the trainee agreed to change his behavior. I waited a full month before contacting the firm again to see how the trainee was doing. They said the talk hadn't done much good because he'd soon returned to his strict schedule. I called the trainee and asked why he was so inflexible. He informed me that he was an avid golfer and that over the last couple of years he had developed the habit of getting in a game of golf in the evenings. He found that if he worked beyond five o'clock in the afternoon, it put him in jeopardy of not getting a tee off time.

I was flabbergasted. This guy, who had gone over two years without gainful employment, didn't see that his rigid attitude, about a hobby was interfering with his chance at a good job with a good company. After a third meeting with the management about his attitude, his connection with the company was severed.

Example 2: I had a fellow working for me when I owned my logging company. He had replaced a worker who had gotten hurt late in the season. We only had about two weeks left until our season ended. He had some hazardous and undesirable work habits that I had spoken to him about on a few occasions but with little subsequent change on his part. I would have replaced him but there weren't any trained people available to take his place. Keeping him almost cost me several thousands of dollars in fines.

We were paid a visit by a safety inspector from the Workers Compensation Board. He was horrified when he watched this man in action. I was able to talk the inspector out of leveling the fines when I told him that the man would not be rehired after the season ended. Luckily for other forestry workers, and ultimately for this man, he never returned to work in the forest industry. It was easier for him to change careers than it was to change his bad work habits.

Proactive or reactive, which are you? Bottom Feeders are reactive. Sharks are proactive. Lets take a look at your history. If you're unemployed right now, tell me why. Was your job loss due to an act of God, war or natural disaster? If it wasn't due to any of these causes, then you might be described as reactive. Were there any signs at all that would indicate that your employment situation was in jeopardy? Was business slowing down? Were any other people being let go? Were any of the top employees finding new opportunities with other employers? Were you now being left out of business activities? Were there more closed-door meetings than before? Were there any recent visits from consultants? Did the company hire someone new in management? Were the competition laying people off? Was there a shift in your responsibilities or were you now doing tasks that were typically below your position? Did they stop asking for your input or informing you of any long-range strategies? Did you ever feel that you were out of the loop?

Sharks prowl their environment with their senses sharp. Because they are always prepared and alert they are seldom someone else's prey. By keeping your skills primed and ready, your resume up-to-date and always on the lookout for a better career opportunity, you will find that you will avoid the rude awakening of having your job pulled out from under you.

"Enough already about being a Shark or being a Bottom Feeder" or "I'd rather be associated with the Bottom Feeders because they are not pushy or boastful," you say. A seminar leader told me after I had chastised him for being too self-promotional, that I was bothered by it because I didn't believe enough in my *own* product. It stopped me in my tracks. He was right.

Modesty is a killer when you're looking for employment. They have a saying in Texas "if you can do it, it ain't bragging!" You had better show some confidence in your product if you want me to buy it or invest in it. Look at any of the products on TV or in the magazines. Do they hold back on describing what they can do for you? Of course not! They have to convince you to buy their product because if they don't, someone else will. I'm not saying that you have to make outrageous claims but if you're good at something, you tell me about it.

If you're good with people, kids, animals, machinery or numbers, then tell me that you're. By informing me what you're good at something doesn't mean that you're claiming to hold any records for it or that you have a room full of trophies at home for that particular trait or skill. If you were not enthusiastic and confident in your product, why would you expect the employer to be?

Think about it. Would you be impressed with a commercial for a new Ford pickup that claimed it wasn't a bad truck and handled pretty well? I doubt it would persuade you to invest thousands of dollars. You'd be much more inclined to put your money into a vehicle that was the number one selling truck for X number years and had won Truck of the Year according to the Pickup People's Magazine. When you're out looking for work, everything that you do is your commercial. Sell me on your product, your benefits and your work ethic.

Not sure why a good work ethic makes you stand out from others? I'll share a story that I heard from Marshall Sylver, motivational speaker and hypnotist. A father asks an employer why his three sons, who all work for the same company, are paid such a wide difference in wages. The employer decided he would let the sons demonstrate the reason for themselves. He told the father to hide and watch.

He summoned the first son. He told him that an airplane had just landed from the Far East. He told him to go down to the airport and find out if there was anything worth buying. The son returned 15 minutes later with his report. He said he phoned the airport and had someone read him the manifest list. The manifest said there was about 100 dozen toy dolls, about 1000 dozen colored pencils and about 500 rolls of fabric. The employer thanked him and dismissed him. He summoned the second son in and gave him the same assignment. The second son returned after 1 1/2 hours. He said he went to the airport and asked to look over the manifest. He decided that there was 135 dozen Taiwanese dolls of medium quality, 2,000 dozen medium quality colored pencils and about 500 rolls of fine fabrics. He thanked the son and dismissed him.

He summoned the third son in and gave him the exact same assignment. He returned well after closing. He said he went out to the airport and asked a crewmember to take him down into the cargo hold so he could inspect the goods. What he found was 135 dozen Taiwanese dolls of adequate quality but not good enough for them to spend too much time and effort on so he contacted their distributor in NY and sold the entire shipment for a quick profit of approximately $ 2000. Next, he found about 2,000 dozen colored pencils of extremely poor quality that was not worth the risk of marketing, so he passed on them. There were supposed to be 500 rolls of fine fabrics but after inspection he decided that only 200 were fine quality. So he sold the 200 to their dealer in San Francisco. Upon further search of the cargo hold, he discovered a last minute addition to the shipment that hadn't been put on the manifest. There was a collection of rare antiques and statuettes of exceptional quality. He contacted a local dealer to confirm his suspicions. The dealer had just verified that they were as valuable as the son thought. He purchased them because they were priced far below market value. He was sure with enough time and the right marketing they could realize a profit of about $100,000. The son said, "you will have my full written report in the morning." The boss thanked the son and dismissed him.

He turned to the father and said, "Your first son didn't even do what he was told. That is why he is paid the least. Your second son does only what he is told. That is why he is paid a bit more. Your third is a rare breed. He does far more than is expected. That is why he is paid far more. Your first two sons are typical of most of my employees and that's why they're dispensable. Your third son has made himself indispensable."

The sign of a Bottom Feeder is only doing what the job requires or less. A Shark will strive, even if it is a job they don't particularly like, to make such a good impression that the employer will be sad to see them go. If you want a great letter of reference then my suggestion would be to earn it.

Chapter 7. A Dynamite Document or a Liner for a Birdcage?

What you're about to experience is an opportunity to sit in on one of my classes. I will share with you the same information that my students receive along with the questions they typically ask me.

Why do I need to have a resume? Why can't it be like the good old days when you just went to a business, filled out an application and they told you to start on Monday? Why do I have to tell them what I'm good at? Can't they just hire me and see how good I'm?

The odd thing about those good old days is that they existed for only a select few. I have worked with thousands of clients and when they talk about the good old days they are telling me how plentiful the jobs were - not for them but for others. It's amazing how selective memories can be. Do you realize that in ten, twenty or thirty years from now, these will be the good old days?

As for hiring you because you showed up, I would bet huge money that many a big company had wished they'd been more selective in their hiring practices. If you were an employer, would you hire the first warm body that came along without at least finding out if that warm body had something to offer?

You're expecting an employer to pay you thousands of dollars per year so you better be able to tell them why they should invest in your services. And there will be plenty of whys. Having worked with yourself, having seen yourself in action, you know what you have to offer an employer. You know the kind of drive, enthusiasm, dedication, initiative, and tenacity that you have to offer but if you don't take the necessary steps to let the employer in on your secret, they may go with someone less qualified. Because of your modesty, you may both lose.

So what's the first step in letting a prospective employer know why you'll be a good candidate for a position? You create a winning resume.

Before you sit down and create a resume, it would help a great deal to understood what a resume is designed to do. Ask the average Bottom Feeder and they will say it is to get you a job. Sorry but that is asking way too much from a piece of paper. The best that a resume can do is to win you an interview. With that in mind, your main focus should be on how to get them interested enough that they'll set aside their precious time to meet you.

Now I've been accused of being cold because I liken a job seeker to a product but that is the cold, hard reality of the situation. You're a product. The employers are the consumers. To win a job, you must convince the customer that your product (you) is the best for them.

Keep this in mind "People only buy two things." I often get someone who takes exception with this idea. They go on to explain that they buy a lot more than only two items. Well it is true - people only buy two things. They buy solutions to problems and they buy good feelings. Think about anything you have ever purchased. It will fall into either category. Here are some examples: do you own a car? Why did you buy it? I'll bet it was because you needed transportation not because you had excess money in the bank and you thought it would be nice to invest in something with a negative return. So when you bought the vehicle, you probably had a budget to work within. Which means you went out and bought the car that gave you the best feeling for the money you could spend.

This question is directed to the female readers but if males feel a need to answer, they are quite welcome. Have you ever bought a dress? For some, you may have had to convince someone else that you actually needed the dress but when you did go out and buy the dress, you bought the one that gave you the best feeling.

Well, it's the same for an employer. Your resume is the solution to their problem. If what you're offering isn't a solution to their problem then it is a worthless document. If you come at your employment search from that angle it will make the entire process much simpler. Do your research. Every business has problems. Figure out how you can solve any one of them and you have yourself an interview. At the interview, they can get the good feeling that you're the right product for them.

I will endeavor to reduce the process of writing an excellent resume that sells you to its simplest form. Not because I think you're not smart enough but because it isn't rocket science.

"What is the difference between junk mail and a brochure?" Think about it. The last time you had a pile of advertisements fill your mailbox, did you throw them all out or did you read any of them? What made you stop and read that particular brochure? Now the answers I typically get to that question are – appearance, they were attractive to look at, interesting, something on them that was of particular interest to the reader, name recognition, they were impressed by the name brand, sales, looked like a good deal.

Well guess what? It's the same with your resume. It will either be treated as a piece of junk mail or a brochure that catches someone's attention. When it comes to appearance, your resume should be attractive enough for the employer to want to read it. It has to be of interest to the employer. Just because you want a job with their company isn't good enough. What is it about you that would make them want to hire you, keep you and invest hard earned training dollars in you? Name recognition doesn't necessarily mean that they recognize your name but they might recognize your education or the skills you're offering. As for sales, I'm not suggesting you offer them two weeks of free work. Your resume should reflect the value you brought to your last employer. How you made an impact there?

There is a common rule that all marketers know and understand and it's a rule that you need to sear into your brain as you create your resume. "You can't sell if you don't match benefits with needs." It doesn't matter how fancy your product is if it doesn't solve my problem. It will remain useless to me. If I'm selling super sucking vacuum cleaners and you have no carpets in your home, it won't matter how powerful it is or how many sucking levels it has because you don't need it. KEEP YOUR FOCUS ON THEIR NEEDS.

Often when people create a resume they break one or more of the following ten most common mistakes.

1. Too long! You've probably heard that your resume should be one page – never more than two. For the most part, I would agree - unless your situation calls for something different. It is asinine to believe that *all* brochures will be limited to either one page or two! There are always exceptions to the rule.

Take, for instance, the current bit of advice with which job seekers are constantly being pelted – your resume should only be one page. What happens if you have a two-page product? Will you be doing yourself any favors by trimming your sales pitch to 50% of its original size? You may have eliminated some very vital information.

I assisted a client with a resume. It was two full pages long, not counting the cover page. She sent it out to ten employers and had eight of them respond to it. It would appear they never had a problem with a two-page resume. On the subject of the infamous one page resume, there has been a major backlash by those having to read the resumes. The most common complaint is that the job seeker, in an attempt to keep the resume to only one page, proceeds to cram two pages of information onto a single sheet of paper. Now the document is a solid block of text and unappealing to read. Yeah, they succeeded in reducing it to the magical one page but no one wants to read it. Seems like a hollow victory. So, put the idea of an ideal length of resume out of your head and focus on making it effective instead.

2. Disorganized. The information is scattered around about the resume without any particular rhyme or reason.

"Why is that a problem?" Most job seekers assume that an employer will take the time to peruse their resumes and find all the gems and nuggets hiding inside. WRONG! The average employer or resume reader will give you less than 30 seconds. This includes your cover letter! To make matters worse, the larger the employer the less time they will spend reading your resume (unless you give them a good reason.) Some of the major businesses or organizations that receive several hundreds of resumes per advertised position will give you between 12 – 20 seconds to sell yourself.

How do you sell yourself in such a short amount of time? Prioritize your information. Look at your resume and ask yourself this question. If I were only allowed to keep only one piece of information from this document to show a prospective employer, what would it be? Once you've decided, write a big number one beside it and repeat the process with the rest of the information.

Here's a bit of employment trivia that might surprise you. In an industry survey of hiring executives, only 4% thought that Education was the most important piece of information. Leading with your education may not be the move for you.

3. Poorly typed and printed. We have heard it all our lives, you've only one chance to make a first impression. That rule applies here too! When an employer receives your resume, it has to be perfect. You will be judged by it contents and appearance.

I had a client come into my office for a copy of his resume. I printed it off and took it from the laser printer. The client and I had not seen each other for quite awhile and took a few moments to get reacquainted. I was amazed and horrified with what followed. As we spoke, he started folding. By the time the conversation was finished that single sheet of paper was reduced to a tiny, folded lump. How many employers would want to keep that wrinkled, folded

Larry Arrance

and manipulated piece of #*!* in their filing cabinet? The answer rhymes with Nero. I've had ex-managers and ex-employers tell me that as soon as the culprit has departed, they thank them for saving them the remaining energy it takes to finish the crumpling and crushing before they toss it into the wastebasket.

Remember, everything about your resume is selling or representing you. If you make it look like a piece of crap, the employer may think the same about you. If you have only a few pieces of trivial information on it, the employer may erroneously believe that you have very little to offer. This document you're handing out can mean the difference between winning a great employment opportunity or staying home and watching the bills pile up.

4. Overwritten. Long paragraphs and sentences. Takes too long to say too little.

Sometimes we are so eager to impress someone with our qualifications that we go too far. Have you heard of the acronym KISS? Keep it simple, stupid. There is a reason for it. Stupid has to read your resume. Stupid has to understand what it is you're trying to say. Now don't get me wrong, I'm not saying that the employer or the human resource s department is stupid. The object here is to communicate, not to intimidate. It is amazing how many job seekers, in their quest to impress the reader, will get out a thesaurus and look for the biggest words possible to describe what they have done. This technique often backfires because you may come across as a pompous, overqualified windbag, or a threat to a supervisor's job because you may seem to be much smarter, or like some schmuck who tried desperately to inflate their resume. A lot of people don't know that the best use of a thesaurus is to find a simpler word to replace a big word.

On the same topic, do not deliver your information in large blocks of text. If the reader sees what appears to be a small mountain of text challenging them to dig in to find the rewards, they will probably toss it aside and look for something easier to digest. So, whenever possible, give them the vital information in point form. The information is a lot easier to consume in nice bite size pieces.

5. Too Sparse. Gives only dates and job titles. Too many resumes are what I call shopping list resumes. They give the company name, dates worked and a list of responsibilities and duties.

There are over 25,000 different occupations in this country alone. Why do so many people figure that because *they* know what *they* did on the job, that the *reader* will know what they did on the job? Do they believe that everyone else is a psychic? What if you received a brochure for a vacuum cleaner and the only they told you about it, was that it sucked. Would they have given you enough reason to hear more about the product?

Tell me what you have to offer because I won't invest precious interview time in the hope that you've kept, some really cool stuff secret that I can pry out of you.

It would be much easier for me to call people who have told me about benefits they could bring to my company.

6. Not Results oriented. Doesn't show what you accomplished.

These resumes remind me of the sheet of information stuck on the window of a new car. Most of the information is useless, unless the reader already knows why the particular piece of information is good for them.

When someone writes on their resume that they held receptionist duties or handled the responsibilities of a certain position, my response is "so what?" You haven't sold me anything. For all I know, you could have been dreadful at it. All you've told me is that you did it, not how successful you were.

Do all sales people sell the same amount? Are there some people in your industry that work harder than others, produce more than others? Of course there is but how would I be able to tell by looking at their resumes? Give me numbers. Quantify the impact that you had on the job.

"What do numbers accomplish?" They will create sharper images in my mind. They let me get my head around what you actually did. Lots of people will write on their resumes that they supervised staff. Did that create much of picture in my mind? Nope. How many did they supervise? There is a huge difference in the level of skills required and the amount of responsibility shown between someone who supervises 1 person and someone who supervises 20 people.

If you tell me you increased sales or business, then you had better tell me by how much. If you did public speaking, how big were the crowds? As a chambermaid, how many rooms did you clean in a day? Quantify, quantify, quantify!

Another benefit of using numbers is that they catch the eye. The natural tendency of the reader is to slow down and read the information surrounding the numbers. This expands the amount of time that your information is in front of the reader's eyes.

7. Too Much Irrelevant Information. Don't confuse them with height, weight, sex, marital status, and other useless information.

There is an FM radio station that every employer listens to while they peruse your resume. It is the same radio station that you're tuned to throughout the day. It is WII-FM. It stands for "What's In It For Me?" You think that I'm exaggerating. Don't you? If you were to take a break right now and go sit in front of your TV, one of the first things you would do is pick up the remote. You'd start flicking through the channels until you found one of interest to you. For curiosity's sake, try this and time yourself on how long you give each program or channel to intrigue you before moving on.

The same thing happens with the employers. The only thing they are interested in on your resume is how can this person make them money, save them money, save them time, or make their life better? Too many people waste precious resume space with stuff that is of no interest to anyone but themselves.

Imagine that you're hiring me to write your resume. I will be charging $1,000 per line. It's a great deal. I highly recommend it. Your job now is to go through your existing resume and decide if it sells a thousand dollars worth of your product. If it doesn't, throw it away.

Let's take a look at some examples. Lots of people will put this word at the top of the page – RESUME. I guess it is put there to prevent the reader from thinking it's a comic book or perhaps a menu. These people might like to see publishers write "Book" on the outside of a book so that there isn't any confusion as to what it is. Here is the first test of the rule: does that word or statement sell a thousand dollars worth of your product? No, so get rid of it.

What about education? How many resume templates (by the way I detest templates because they are so limiting) start your resume with your education? Remember, you're supposed to start with your strongest sell. What if education isn't your strongest card to play? I have seen people claiming they graduated high school in 1963. What have they sold me? Age, that's all. I would bet money that their work history is a lot more valuable to me than what they've forgotten from grade 12. Or how about when someone tells me that they completed grade 10, what have they sold me? Yeah, that they didn't finish high school. The key to including your schooling - is only if it sells.

Some people like to include every course they've ever taken. Ensure that I see the relevance. When you see someone has taken a Stress Management course, what might you think? I had a client that thought it would be interesting to take an Anger Management course. When you hear someone has taken that type of course, what do you think? That's right, they were forced to take it because they have a problem. If it isn't a selling point, get it off the paper.

What about those people who have a great deal of post-secondary education to their credit? Is it necessary for them to include their high school information? Isn't a safe assumption that if you completed university or college, that you should have your high school diploma? You will only accomplish dating yourself.

I always get questions concerning what to put into a Job Objective. This is a sensitive subject because I know people who are enamored with them. I'm not one of them. Too many job objectives that I've seen have become a barrier instead of an invitation for the reader to read further. Unfortunately, many resume writers are so focused on what they want from the employer that they feel bound and determined to tell them right up front. Some of the Job Objectives I have seen are as follows:

To obtain a suitable position – (lame) how many people are looking for an unsuitable position?
To obtain permanent, full time work in the computer industry. Too many parameters for the employer. Does this mean you would not consider part-time, temporary, seasonal, or contract work?
To obtain a position in retail, hospitality, the service industry or construction. It appears you don't care where you work. If you come across as an *anything* worker, then I may assume you'll jump at the next *anything* that comes along.
To obtain a position that will allow me to grow and offers training and continued growth. Sounds impressive but who pays for training? It doesn't seem very wise start your sales pitch by putting your hand into the employer's pocket looking for training dollars.
To obtain an awarding position. Does this mean I have to give them trophies from time to time? I asked the young woman who had put this on her resume, why? She said someone else suggested it because it sounded good to them. Great, let them put it on theirs.

I'm not saying you can't put an objective on your resume. My recommendation is to use an objective that offers something to the employer. Would I use a job objective on my resume? No! An employer would know what job I was after because I would have told them in my cover letter.

Quite a few resumes will have this on the bottom of the page "References available upon request." Don't get me wrong, there is nothing wrong with finishing your resume with this but if it came down to putting this line in or selling me something I can use, sell me the something I can use. Any intelligent company is going to ask you for references whether you say they are available or not.

So when you go through your resume, make sure the information meets this single most important criteria: does it sell you? I don't care what any of the so-called resume experts say. If the information doesn't sell you, it serves no purpose.

8 – Mistakes in spelling and grammar. All it takes is one misplaced letter and your meaning is completely changed. I work with some very talented people but sometimes a mistake can slip through. One of my associates is a skilled typist who is very fast on the keyboard. She was typing up a cover letter that a client had given her. In the cover letter, the client was informing the prospective employer that they would prefer to have "nightshifts". In her haste, the typist omitted the letter "f." Does that change the message the author was trying to convey? Now all of a sudden the employer is trying to understand why this individual would want to share such personal information. Perhaps he'll think the applicant is trying to promote his dedication he by having this condition only in the evenings so that it won't interfere with his work.

With the advent of the computer and word processor, many of us have become dependent upon "Spellchecker." Is Spellchecker perfect? No, and the users are not either. I consistently get "form" and "from" mixed up. Will Spellchecker have a problem with either of these two words? No, but they will not convey the correct message. My suggestion to ensure that each word is spelled correctly is to take the finished document and read it backwards. (No, that does not mean facing the other way.) Start at the bottom of the page and read to the top. There will be no logical flow to the words and if a word is wrong, it should jump out at you.

Surveys have shown that 45% of employers will eliminate you from the job competition because of a typographical error. I believe we need to put that number into perspective. It would depend what kind of position you were after before an employer would penalize you. If you're going after a janitorial or construction position, the odd typo shouldn't spell your doom. If, on the other hand, you were going after a clerical position, it is safe to assume that the number of employers who would disqualify you because of single typo is probably closer to 100%. After all, typing would be what you would be doing for them, isn't it? So, a sloppily prepared document would be a perfect example of what they could expect from you.

9. Tries too hard. This includes fancy typesets, too many different fonts and font sizes, exotic paper stock, pictures, and gimmicks.

Yes, the advice that you should stand out from the crowd is good advice but your efforts should still make sense. There are many stories of people utilizing creative and, sometimes, bizarre techniques to get their resumes read. Keep in mind that just because something worked once doesn't mean it will work for everyone. I heard of a fellow who attached his resume to a pizza box and had the pizza delivered to the human resource manager. Unfortunately, this method only worked once because others have because tried pizzas, cakes and fruit baskets and came up short for their efforts.

I've also heard that a professional from the employment search industry promotes the use of downloading a corporation's logo and putting it on your resume. Because it worked for his teenage daughter, and he thinks he's hit on a brilliant strategy. When I surveyed several employers about such a bold move, they gave it a big thumbs down. They wondered what would be the next move, stalking them at home?

Forget all the glitz and glamour and focus on showing them that you have what they need. When you're choosing a font keep to the more accepted styles. Times New Roman may seem boring to some but it is easy to read and that is what is most important. Be careful of using too many different font sizes. It makes for very unpleasant reading because it creates excessive work for the eyes.

Some job seekers believe they'll have better luck if they use wildly colored paper or place their resume inside a binder of some sort. First off, with colored paper, you're taking a risk because the employer maybe turned off by that color or perhaps they'll think that you're normally flamboyant and a show off. Is that the image you want them to have of you? Also, they may think you're trying to cover up a lack of content by using fancy paper.

It was once a trend for job seekers to attach a photograph of themselves to their resume. Imagine that you're an employer and you receive a resume with a person's picture attached - a picture that you never requested. What do you think? I've asked many employers and managers. A common response is the person's vanity comes into question. Do they actually think that their face will be a deciding factor in the hiring process? By sending a picture, you may create an opportunity to be discriminated against. What if they don't like your face? I know, some people say "what's the difference, you're taking your face to the interview anyway?" It does make a big difference because when you deliver your face in person, you're there to sell yourself.

10. No connection to the position sought. It is amazing how people will just pop into a business and drop off a resume or mail or fax it in without any means for the receiver to figure out what position they are pursuing. The company may assume the person lacks the smarts or the backbone to pick up a telephone and ask for information. Employers consider neither of those two attributes desirable.

Larry Arrance

Chapter 8. You'll Make Them Smile When You've Got the Right Style.

I chuckle when a students asks, "What's the best way to write a resume?" They are immensely disappointed that there isn't one concrete way to write a resume. Why would anyone think there was? If I have eighteen students in my class, none of them should have the same resume. There are eighteen different products. There should be eighteen different *brochures*.

I'll share with you some of the basic styles, advantages and disadvantages. Choose the format that best sells your product. By all means, feel free to take the best of any or all of them and design a *brochure* that best suits your needs.

RESUME STYLES

This first resume style is called "Chronological" because it features the dates of your past employment. It is a very standard format but it has a history of being misused. The only time I would consider using a basic chronological resume is if I was staying in the same industry. The chronological resume focuses on two main pieces of information. First, it sells your last position. This isn't a problem unless you're changing careers. I worked with a female client who had a pretty solid career in administration working with computers. She had an opportunity to leave that career and spend some time on a ranch as a ranch hand. She had her fill of life on a ranch, she decided to get back into the clerical field. She went seeking employment utilizing a chronological resume.

I want you to imagine that you're seeking an employee to fill a position behind your computer. You receive a resume. The first job on the resume reads "Ranch hand". What pictures are going through your mind? Cowboys, horses, denim, cowboy boots, and cow pies? It's hard to imagine this person behind your computer. She had little interest from employers when using this resume. We converted her resume to a "Functional" style, which I will talk about in a moment.

The second piece of information the chronological resume brings to an employer's attention is the dates of employment. If you have any gaps in your employment history, you as well have waved a big red flag and said, "Here is a problem!" If you include months as part of your date, you have just encouraged your reader to do the math to see how long you went between jobs. My suggestion is to eliminate months and stick with years. You can always go into details at the interview. By dropping the months, you now eliminate a short-term position that may not look good on your work history.

The benefits of a chronological resume are that they are quick and easy for the employer to read. The downfall is that it tends to sell the last job or become repetitive if you have done the same type of work with many employers. As I stated previously, I'd only use a chronological style is if I was staying within the same industry.

If you have gaps in your work history or you're changing careers, you will want to focus an employer's attention on things that will put you in a much more favorable light. You're going to want to promote skills and abilities that they can utilize. This is called a "functional" or "skill based" resume.

With a functional resume, you have a little more freedom and flexibility. When determining the skills you're going to highlight for an employer, consider the key skills the industry or position requires. Then, cluster the appropriate examples of those skills into categories that make sense for that position. When deciding what should be included in the lists, keep in mind that a skill is a skill is a skill. It doesn't matter whether you picked it up from work experience, school, correspondence course, volunteer experience, or as a homemaker. All that matters is that you have the skill. When you're packaging your skills, the groupings are pretty much up to your imagination. They can be job title categories such as cook, plumber or technician. Another option is to lump them into sections with headings like Organizational, Interpersonal or Supervisory.

By choosing to sort your skills in one, two, three, four or five sections, you can eliminate the repetitiveness so often found in chronological resumes. If you have had several jobs in the same industry, there is a great likelihood that you had many of the same duties. How excited would you be to read the same piece of information over and over? So why would you do it to someone you're trying to impress? Every line on your resume should be offering the employer another reason for acquiring your product.

Lots of clients have asked me if they can just list their skills and abilities and not mention their work history. I don't recommend that because not mentioning where you acquired or demonstrated those skills, they may become very suspicious. The people that ask me this often have a very sketchy work history and are looking for ways to disguise that fact. Many so-called experts may try to steer you away from the functional resume stating that they are too general or have the one-size-fits-all feel about them. I don't think that needs to be the case. If you make every line sell your product, the reader won't care about the style.

"Combination" resumes are just that. They combine both strengths of the chronological and functional resumes. They begin with a shorter selection of skills and abilities than you would find in a full-fledged functional, followed by a pared down version of a full-fledge chronological. They can be very effective - if done properly. If done without much effort, you will suffer the fate of most combination products. They are not enough of either to make your sale. Think of some of the products that have come into the marketplace throughout the years that have tried to be more than one thing at a time. I remember a huge combination TV, radio and stereo phonograph (wow, did I just age myself with that one.) The combination seldom performed well in any of the categories.

The fourth, and one of my favorites, is the "enhanced chronological" resume. This is much like a typical chronological except it has the Shark mentality. It hits you hard with the successes and achievements you've demonstrated throughout your career. There is nothing modest about this resume. It doesn't settle by stating that you were part of successful team. It will state exactly the role you played and what the outcome was. It won't just establish that you increased sales, it will proclaim loud and clear what the figures or percentages were. With it's every breath, it will scream that you're a winner! It will proudly herald your achievements and the impact you had on previous employers.

If you already have a resume, take it out and let's rebuild it. Start at the top and put a check mark next to anything you believe is critical to selling your product. Anything else can be looked at later. Look over your critical list. Is the benefit to the employer obvious enough that we can leave it alone? Be brutally honest with yourself. If it isn't clear what the benefit is, then make it clear. Tell them about skills you've developed or demonstrated. When you look at the non-critical information, ask yourself why it's good for the employer. What skills or abilities does it highlight? Do not hesitate to tell them. They do not have the time or the energy to guess what the benefit is; you on the other hand, do have the time and energy to tell them.

If any piece of information does not have a clear benefit, get rid of it. It doesn't sell you.

You may have heard of a scannable resume. Relax. They're not hard to create. Take your regular resume and start undoing. Undo the bolding, underlining, bullets, boxes or any dressing up. A scanner is a machine that electronically scans the resume for pertinent information. This is part of the culling process. The scanner goes over your resume first before a human set of eyes takes a closer look. What the scanner will be looking for are key words that a company considers critical for this position. It will not matter how beautifully you have written your resume. If it does not find those key words it will come up with **NOTHING!** Your resume will be eliminated from consideration. Take a copy of your resume, dress it down and save it as your scannable resume. Don't worry that it isn't a piece of art because your competition's resume won't be either.

If you don't have a resume, take out a piece of paper and do what I call Verbal Vomit. Write down absolutely every detail about every job or volunteer position you have ever held. Don't worry if they are not connected or in any specific groups. Just get it down. It's amazing that by putting down one piece of information can spark your memory to bring up even more information. Once you have it all down, go through and group items together into skills and abilities or assign them to the job in which you acquired or demonstrated them.

Highlights of qualifications or summaries can work as great teasers at the beginning of a resume. They generally consist of four or five bulleted features that are key selling points to catch an employer's interest. It could state number of years in an industry, educational and trade level achieved, or characteristics or abilities needed for a certain position. Note: if you're using numbers associated with experience, don't use too many of them. I've had clients with extensive experience where some of the skill areas or jobs overlapped. By listing the years from each category, an employer may add them up and assume you're very old. Don't assume they automatically know what you're talking about. Tell them.
We have a saying in this industry. "Your resume is either a winner or a killer." The choice is yours.

Many job seekers are supplementing their resumes by building their own web page. Before you panic, they are much easier to build than you think. There is a site on the Internet called Freecenters.com that will provide a free web page. Most will have simple step-by -step approaches to create an eye catching and effective web page. It can be used to enhance a scannable resume or a resume you email. Include a link or address to your web page on your resume. Make sure that you display only relevant information.

Now that I've shown you some samples of resume styles, I have another question for you. "When is the right time to write a resume?" Some of you may be thinking, in the morning? Or maybe after a good meal? Sure, those are both good times but the best time to write a resume is when you're still working. Why? Because when you're working, you feel better about your product. You're likely to see yourself in a much more positive light. It can be startling how fast self-esteem drops once you've lost your job.

So my advice to you is: When you get your next job, start revamping your resume. I want you to make a note in your daytimer or on your calendar to revisit your resume in three months. After three months, revamp and update your resume. This will keep the resume current and ready to go. If you take out your resume and can't think of anything new to add to it, I will find out and I will track you down. Why will I be upset with you? Because if you have nothing new to add after three months, it means you have done nothing to make your product more marketable. You have not taken on any new challenges or responsibilities. You have not taken any courses that will make you more valuable. Basically, you will be telling me that you've enjoyed previous bouts of unemployment because you're using the best-known path to losing a job. It's called *Apathy*. It's amazing how many people give up control over their career to an employer, manager or supervisor. I've got some tough news for those people. There is only one person's career that they're concerned with - and it isn't yours.

I had a client tell me that getting fired was the best thing that ever happened to him because it showed him, quite drastically, what happens when you give away control of your career. From that moment on, he put himself at the helm of his career. Some experts suggest that you become a career activist and spend about 20% of your time preparing yourself for your next employment opportunity. This means keeping your skills up to date and, or acquiring new skills and the ability to market them to potential employers.

When I tell this to my students, I often get someone saying they pride themselves on the loyalty they display to their employers. That's admirable but potentially dangerous to your career. Keep in mind that this is your career and there will only be one person who will be loyal to it. And that person is you. If your company is forced into cutting staff, how loyal will they be to you? They have to be loyal to their bottom line. That's just business. If a better opportunity comes up for you, give it serious consideration. Don't worry about how your present employer can survive without you because they CAN survive without you. Consider that your leaving the company may create a wonderful opportunity for someone else.

Larry Arrance

Chapter 9. Cover Me I'm Going In!

"What's the big deal with cover letters?" You say you have never used one before or if you did it was merely to tell the employer that there was a resume attached. Did you actually say that or are you doing your best Bottom Feeder impression? As many as 60% percent of employers say that the cover letter is as important as, and in many cases more important than, the resume. A good cover letter is a very powerful sales device that creates a desire for the employer to meet you. Unlike the resume, which should be fact-based and statistical, the cover letter can give an employer a glimpse into your personality. It can give you an opportunity to express enthusiasm and interest while offering your multitude of services to their organization.

I liken the cover letter's relationship with a resume to a recipe and the picture of the finished dish. You might be interested in a recipe by reading it but the interest rate soars when you see a mouthwatering picture of the dish in lush, vivid colors. Your cover letter should accomplish the same thing. It should whet the appetite of the reader and encourage them to examine your resume in greater detail.

I'll share a story with you about how powerful an impact a cover letter can have on a person's job search. A client came in to our office on a Monday. She was dragging her feet and looking very defeated. I asked her why she was so down. She told me that she had phoned into a local radio talk show the day before and had been told some very discouraging things. Her story went on to say that the host and his guest of the day, both self-proclaimed experts on the subject of employment issues, informed her and the listening audience that because of her age and qualifications she would never find work in our fair city.

Needless to say, I wasn't impressed with the level of compassion and support they had offered her. I said, "Let me take a look at what you have been handing out to employers." After reviewing her resume, I informed her that although it wasn't the best I had ever seen it was still pretty good. When she showed me her cover letter I saw her problem. It was weak and didn't say anything of consequence. I took it from her and told her I would revamp it for her. When I handed it back to her, she said "Wow! I'd hire me." She faxed off three cover letters and resumes to job postings that afternoon. She called me about an hour and a half later to inform me that she had two interviews set for the next day. Within the next two weeks, she had sixteen interviews using the same resume but also including a powerful cover letter. Luckily for this lady, I was able help her prove how wrong the two professionals were.

I know of many employers that don't bother to read resumes that come without a cover letter attached. For some it's because they know it takes more effort to create a cover letter for them and this help to screen out the bottom feeders that wander around dropping the same resume to every employer on the block. Other employers want to see a cover letter to get some idea of your written communication skills. Unlike the resume, which is usually written with the information in list or point form, the cover letter will showcase proper sentence structure. So, just like the resume, the cover letter can be a marvelous screening tool.

"Does every job need one?" No, if you have been in the same industry, like construction, and you're applying for another laboring position then a good pair of boots and decent resume should be all you need. But if you're going for any kind of a career change, then it is probably job seeker suicide to attempt it without a good cover letter. My rule of thumb is "Only use a cover letter for the jobs you want." That should keep it simple for you.

"What are some uses for a cover letter?" Some people have had trouble reducing their resume to a nice even two pages or one page. They have two pages and a bit or one page and a bit. The cover letter can be used to slice that extra part off and used when necessary. Remember how I mentioned earlier that I'm not a huge fan of job objectives on a resume? This is because I can go into much more detail in a cover letter as to what I'm looking for and why it is a good thing for an employer. A good cover letter can make it clearer than your resume as to exactly why you're right for a position.

Beside the few uses for the cover letter that I mentioned above, the real purpose for the letter is to make a connection to the job that you're applying for. Several years ago one of the key personal components to our office left to pursue her career in another portion of the country. This left a pretty big role to fill. She had been a dynamite facilitator and a very successful office manager. My employers placed ads in the papers for a replacement. I was not a part of the hiring decision and as such I had no reason to go through the 177 resumes that came in for the position. The opportunity to see the resume of the young woman who eventually won the position came after she had actually been hired.

When I looked over her resume, I could not for the life of me, figure out why she even got an interview, let alone won the position. Remember we were looking for someone to fill the position of Facilitator and Office Manager. This young lady had five years of university in her chosen field and had worked for two years in that field. She was a Public Health nurse. What the heck did that have to do with teaching job search classes and running an office? When I had the chance to read her cover letter it became clear. Throughout her cover letter, she created connections from her education, work experience and personality that showed she was ideal for the position. When I reread her resume, I knew where to look and how to look at it. That is what a cover letter should do.

"What is the best format for a cover letter?" The answer is the same when they asked about a resume. There isn't one. Format is not as important as content. Your only concern should be: is it appealing, does it have impact and can it be read quickly?

Does it make the reader sit up and take notice? Does it create a desire for the reader to want to meet you? Think of one of your greatest triumphs or achievements that is related to the position you're going after and tell them about it. Show where you have had impact for your past employers. Show them that you have a history of being valuable and they will figure that you could be valuable for them too. Besides making them want to read your resume, you had better make it readable. Remember that people, who understand big words, understand little words. People who only understand little words only understand little words. I seriously doubt if you have had to look up any of the words I've used so far and I'll bet you have appreciated that. Keep your writing clean and crisp. Your sentences will have greater impact if you keep them short. If there is a way to cut one long sentence into two, do it.

Now, I mentioned that there isn't one basic cover letter format but the cover letters can be broken down into 4 categories.

Invited cover letter. Where would you see the invitation? In the advertisement or posting. The benefits of invited cover letters are that they can go into detail about the advertised position. This makes it very easy for you because all you have to do is tell them how good a fit you could be for the company's opening. The downfall of the invited cover letter is the fact that everyone else has seen the invitation and the competition can be fierce. This is the only type of cover letter that a Bottom Feeder knows.

Uninvited cover letter. It may uninvited but not, necessarily, unwanted. Sharks searching out opportunities that have not been listed use Uninvited letters. The benefit of the uninvited cover letter is that there may not be any competition. You might be the only job seeker approaching this company. The other benefit is that because you're up close and personal and doing your own research, you will most likely have a name to use. Many ads or postings, don't have anyone specific to address your cover letter to. Sharks prefer to create their own opportunities rather than wait for an employer to post a job.

Referral cover letters. These are by far the most powerful and influential of the three. They work because you included in the body of your cover letter is the name of someone the reader knows and, hopefully, respects. Do not underestimate the power of using someone's name. Stop and look at the ads on television. Advertising companies spend millions of dollars every year to have celebrities endorse their products. Why? It works. We attach our good feelings about the celebrity to the product they are hawking. The same holds true for using someone's name in your cover letter. They will attach whatever feelings they have for that person to you. It is very powerful. Do not hesitate to use it.

Generic cover letter. Generally this type of cover letter does not convey quality. You get a sense that it is connected to a product that was designed for the mass market. Do not be guilty of sending out these mass handouts that don't say anything of value and are a terrible waste of paper. Research the name of whoever you're sending the cover letter to. You know yourself when you receive a letter in the mail and it isn't addressed to you, you're not impressed. When you receive a letter with your name attached, even though you know your name may have been pumped out by a computer program, you appreciate it. You will give it more attention than the dreaded *Occupant* or *Dear Sir or Madam.*

It was stated as one of the keys to winning friends and influencing people - use their name. It's the sweetest word in their vocabulary. In today's world of instant information, thanks to the telephone and Internet, it is usually a simple matter of finding out someone's name. When that isn't possible, do not resort to the mind numbing and often irritating "To Whom It May Concern or the Dear Sir or Madam." I can tell you right now that no one will be *concerned* and you haven't done yourself any favors by acknowledging that they are one of the two genders. If you don't know to whom to address your letter, then think it through. Larger companies will probably have a Human Resources Department and you can address your letter to them. Smaller companies will have a manager or hiring authority, so that's the title I put in. If you're not sure and don't want to risk offending someone, don't not put in a salutation line at all. Imagine the appreciation from the readers when you don't force them to read filler lines. They will just dive right into your powerful letter.

Powerful cover letters are powerful for one reason only. They address the Greed Gland of the employers. Remember the employers has only one thing on their minds when they read your cover letter, what's in it for them? Think about what they want, what are their concerns and then give it to them. I had a client that had applied for a pilot's position with a major airline. He showed me the resume and cover letter he had sent to them. I read it and turned to face him. I said "Let's imagine that you're hiring a pilot for a position with *your* airline. What would you want to know about this person? What do you think are key qualities and attributes to be a successful hire for the airline? He went on to answer those questions. I then pointed to his cover letter and asked him to show me where those things were in his letter. Most of what he had written would have sent up red flags if I were the employer.

He had focused on his strong connection to the community and his involvement with volunteer activities. He went to great lengths to promote his love of his church and family and how much he likes taking part in activities that promote a happy, healthy home life. I know those are all admirable but my concern when I hire a pilot is that I will be sending him away from home. That is what pilots do. They fly away. My concern would be that his connections wouldn't allow him the freedom to take longer flights or that we'd have to schedule him around his activities. My suggestion is to go through your resume and ask yourself is this good for me or is it good for them. If it's good for you, throw it away. If it's good for them, keep it.

One of my clients handed me a two-page cover letter. I did what most employers wouldn't do - I read it. A word to the wise: if it looks like a novel, it won't get read. This client had missed the point altogether. All through the two pages he kept telling the prospective employers how much he expected from them. He went on to state that they could acquire his services for $500 per day or $75-85 per hour. It was me, me, me all the way through it! Another client had a very strong religious conviction, and all the power to her. It does not belong in the cover letter. She began her letter with "By the grace of God, when you hire me, I will be able to do this, that and the other thing for my eight and ten year old children." Even if she was applying to a church, she should be telling them what she could do for them and not the other way around. The church has lots of charities to donate to; they do not need another one. And by introducing children, you've just warned them that you have two money pits and possible distractions that might prevent you from doing your job or being satisfied with the wages. So write this down and keep it somewhere prominent. *"They're only interested in what you can do for them, not what they can do for you."*

You would not believe how many cover letters I've read that started out with "I recently moved here from (Name of other place) with my husband and three children." Dial 1-800-WHO CARES. Why are you

109

telling me that information? All you've accomplished is pointing out that you're from somewhere else and you're an outsider. As an employer, I now have to worry that you may be transient and there might be another move in your future. You have also brought your family into the picture. This may not be so good because I may be concerned about possible daycare problems or other distractions that come with raising children.

"What should you focus on?" What do they need to know? Why should they pick you over the other contestants? There are risks involved with hiring new employees. Your job is to reduce any possible risks and replace them with the rewards that come with hiring you. What are your accomplishments related to the position you're going after? If you think you don't have any, then think again. Did you do something that would demonstrate people, management, interpersonal, customer service or communication skills that are similar to what is needed for the position? Think of three key qualities or character traits that describe your work ethic and are necessary for success in this position. For example - conscientious, caring and customer service oriented. Now give me examples that would show you have those qualities.

There's your basics on writing a cover letter. In the next chapter, I'll show you ways to have them scrambling to the phone to arrange an interview.

Chapter 10. Taking it from a Letter to a Lethal Weapon.

My idea of a good cover letter is one that creates fear. Fear that someone else will snap up the product before they even get a chance at looking at it.

"How do you make your cover letter stand out from the rest?" There are some definite tricks or if you prefer devices that a Shark will use to hold the reader's attention of guide their eyes to key information. Your most important psychological weapon to deploy will be your opening paragraph. You have to catch my attention. Imagine if I'm a manager or employer and I have had the opportunity or bad luck to sift through a stack of resumes and cover letters. After reading a number of letters that start with "I'm writing you this letter…or your advertisement said you were looking for…please accept this resume as" they will have slipped into a near coma induced by boredom. Your opening line has to snap them out of their stupor. I recently read a novel that began with "The doctor is here to see you. That's when I knew I was dead." Okay, it got my attention because those two sentences don't usually go together. This is called a hook. Every good sales device uses one.

Getting the reader to sit up and take notice can be accomplished in a number of ways.
Use a technique that instructors and public speakers incorporate to hold your attention. If I ask you a

question, which I have been doing all along, you will be answering them. Maybe not out loud but you will be answering them inside your head. That is human nature. So start with a question. Ask them what quality is the hardest to find in a new employee. Then suggest several very obvious traits that you know are key to this position. Your second paragraph is dedicated to demonstrating why you're all those things you mention in the first paragraph.

You can also start with a quotation from a famous person related to the field that you applying for. You can't go too far wrong quoting Ben Franklin or Albert Einstein. Another eye-catching technique is to use a bold statement to begin you pitch. Tell them about a major achievement that screams that you're a success. Remember when I suggested that you identify three key qualities about your work ethic? To make them work even better for you, tell me what they are and change their font by bolding it and putting in an italicized style.

If you look in most books that describe how to write a cover letter you will see a basic theme. The formula for the cover letter is broken down into I Have, I Can and I'm. Generally there will be three paragraphs. First paragraph deals with I have, which means you will be sharing information as to your qualifications for the job. This could mean training, education, certificates or experience. The second paragraph concerns itself with information declaring what you can do and what you have done. Telling them whether you can sell, teach, build, design, serve or operate a piece of equipment, etc. The third paragraph is dedicated to information about yourself as a person. Things dealing with personality traits like punctuality, team player or dedicated.

The tendency for writing a cover letter is to write it from the 'I' perspective. This is natural unfortunately it makes for lousy reading. It is appalling how many cover letters are given to me to critique that are saturated with the word 'I'. Sometimes every sentence begins with I. I did this. I'm that. I'm a cat in a hat. Do you see what kind of reading this is for the employer? Not only does it come across as egotistical, it is also very clumsy reading that pushes your reader away from you. To bring your reader into your letter you need to incorporate lots of 'You' or 'Yours' into the writing. Instead of telling them "I have seven years of experience in sales and customer service" say, "You will appreciate my seven years of experience in sales and customer service." Do this and you will make your cover letter easier and more enticing to read. You can still use I to start the odd sentence but don't overdo it.

"Have you ever received a letter of any kind?" That might seem like a goofy question but I say that because with the invention of email, letters are becoming something from our past. Did the letter have a PS on the bottom? Did you read it? Unless you're different then 99% of the rest of us, you did read it. Take advantage of this device. What will happen is the reader will see the PS and go immediately to the blurb and read it. Then they will go up and read the letter and finish with reading the PS again. If you want them to know something key about you, put it in the PS. They will see it twice.

"Won't I turn them off if I sound like I'm bragging or boasting?" This is a huge concern for most of my clients. I want you to watch the commercials on TV. Do they hold back at all as to what they can do for you? Of course not, they want you to put out hard earned dollars to buy their product. Would you be inclined to shell out your money if they don't make you feel like they are the answer to you problem? Not likely! So why is it any different with your product? Instead of saying you have Customer Service experience tell them that you have a proven history of capturing and keeping customers. Which one gives the impression of being you being a dynamic results oriented asset for their business?

Bottom Feeders will waste a reader's time by telling them that they have attached a resume and the information is in it. Well DUH Einstein! They can see that there is a resume attached. Tell them why they need to read the resume. I know of employers who will not even glance at the resume if you haven't turned them on in the cover letter. If you feel obliged to mention there is a resume attached, write Encl. or Attached at the bottom. They will know what that means.

I do a little exercise in class where I will choose one of the women and use her as the example. I do this because I'm a man and it is more comfortable for me to say it out loud to a woman. I'll ask her "Simone, imagine you go home tonight and your significant other says to you, Simone I FEEL I love you. Simone I THINK I love you. Simone I BELIEVE I love you. Or, Simone I KNOW I love you. Which one of those statements has the biggest impact for you?" Obviously, she picks the KNOW statement. My question is the same to you. Which statement would carry the most impact for you if you were an employer: I FEEL I have what you need, I THINK I would make a good addition to your team, I BELIEVE I have the necessary qualifications, I KNOW I'm the best candidate because…? If you're not sure about your worth to the business, why should you expect them to invest thousands of dollars for your product? A very successful businessman told me that if you want to get a client's attention and business "Promise big and deliver big!" Others will tell you to keep your promises small and deliver big and they will be pleasantly surprised. The problem with this is that because your promise was small they decided to go with the product that claimed to offer the most.

Testimonials are some of the most powerful sales techniques used in marketing. If you don't believe me, just take a look at most of the infomercials that hawk billions of dollars worth of products each year. There is nothing like a happy customer telling us about a great product, encouraging us to try it ourselves. You can use your own testimonials, also known as letters of recommendation, references or written job evaluations. Select key pieces from the letters and interject them into your cover letter. This is ideal for those of you who are uneasy bragging about yourself. You can let others do it for you.

When I compose a cover letter for a client, I will put the quotation in italics and enclose them in quotation marks. The reader's eyes are automatically drawn to anything that looks like someone speaking. Of course, you'll have to have copies of the original letters of recommendations to back up your cover letter. They don't need to be attached to the resume. Some people ask why they should do this when it would be simpler to just to attach their letters of reference to the back of the resume. Just because you attached them, doesn't mean someone will read them. It makes more sense to use the best of the letters to encourage them to read the cover letter and resume.

Bigger isn't always better unless we are talking bank accounts. You're going to be told that proper length of a cover letter is one half to three quarters of a page. First off, I hate the cookie cutter approach to anything. Everyone is a different product and thus should have a cover letter the length that best sells them. Length isn't as important as good writing. If the writing is good you won't notice the length of the material. Most of the cover letters I have seen aren't go long enough. Brevity is acceptable if the material you have included sells your product. I composed a resume and cover letter for my wife who was looking for a better position. The cover letter was a full page long and the resume was two full pages in length. She submitted it to ten companies. Eight of them invited her in for interviews. Obviously 80% of them did not have a problem with the length of the resume or cover letter.

"Would they be more impressed with a handwritten cover letter?" A slim segment of the employers might but I wouldn't risk it. Before we talk about the reasons for not writing it by hand (unless they have requested it that way), let's discuss why some might request a handwritten letter. There are three basic reasons for the request. From a handwritten letter, I can discern your communication skills. It should also be pretty obvious as to the quality of your penmanship by how easy it is to read your work. Lastly, and not as common, is that it can be used for analyzing your character.

If they have not requested a letter in writing, don't give them the opportunity to get a wrong impression about you. If I receive a handwritten letter when I'm not expecting one, especially when it concerns something regarding business, I might think that the person is not computer literate. Another thought may be that your approach to things is unprofessional. We are so accustomed to seeing the printed page that it throws us for a bit of a loop to see a handwritten page. Would your belief in the value of this book go down or up if it were all handwritten?

"How do I end my cover letter?" Studies show that we tend to remember the beginnings and endings of things more than the middle. With this in mind, the opening and closing of your cover letter needs to be strong.

That way you can remind them again about the major reason that you would be a success for them. You could leave them with a promise or a teaser such as "Give me one half hour of your time and I will demonstrate why I'm the best candidate for this position."

90% of the people who have come through our offices use the passive approach to finding employment. Passive is the favorite style for Bottom Feeders. They prefer to hint or allude to what they want rather than just coming out and asking for it. Most of the cover letters will end with "You can reach me at…or please feel free to contact me…or I would be interested in an interview." When someone sends me a cover letter that states that I should please feel free to call him or her, I wonder, how long do I have until I make contact? I have forever! There's no pressure on me at all. Have you ever supervised staff? How effective would it be for you to say to them "please feel free to do such and such?" Or maybe you have children and you want them to clean their room, so you say "I would be interested in seeing your room cleaned." Is it likely to get cleaned?

They have a saying in sales. If you want the sale, you have to ask for it. If you want an interview, then ask for it. Our chances of getting something go up by 200% when we ask for it. Some people have problems asking for things. This could stem from growing up in a family or being in a relationship where their every need and whim was fulfilled without ever asking for it. Can you relate to that? I know I can't.

An assertive person will ask for the interview. This is actually very simple. Just write "Please call me or please contact me for an interview or a chance to meet in person." There is no confusion there. Studies show that when you give someone instructions, they are likely to follow them. A Shark will take this situation a higher level. Because they know whom they are targeting with this letter, they are in a position to do follow-up. They state loud and clear that they will follow up the letter with a phone call to ensure it was received and to answer any questions. Give them the time of week that you will be making the contact. This gives them ample time to respond to your letter. I have taught enough stress management workshops to know that your stress level goes up according to the lack of control you feel in a situation. To reduce your stress level, make sure you make the follow up call. What is the worst that can happen when you make your call? The position might be gone already. But at least you know and you don't need to waste any more energy on it.

"Should I include the times when I can be reached?" Restrictions for the employers are seldom beneficial. When you restrict the times that you can be contacted to certain hours or times of the day, it can work against you. One of my clients created enormous stress for herself by establishing that she could be contacted between 9:00 am and 3:00 pm Monday to Friday. She would come in hustling and bustling to squeeze as much job search activities into the short time available before we closed our offices for the day. I finally asked her why she waited so late in the day to use our services. When she told me how she had handcuffed herself to the phone for such a major portion of the day, I started to laugh. I explained there was a reason why answering machines were invented or why some people will use a cellular phone. There are few positions that an employer needs to fill on such a short notice that they can't afford to leave a message for a prospective employee. To be truly effective as a job seeker you need to be out the majority of the day connecting with employers not sitting at home nervously watching the phone.

Finally, what kind of a salutation should I use? There are the standards like *becauserely* and *yours truly*. Either of them is fine. I had one client who liked the term "Yours in good business." Judging by the response he got, I don't think it was all that influential. I heard of one woman who finished her letter with "Eventually yours." She landed the job. I can't be sure but maybe the subliminal message filtered through to the employer. It doesn't matter as long as you leave room to sign your name. Oh, and on that note, make sure if you're handing the letter off in person or sending it via the mail, that you sign it in blue ink. If you use black ink, it will look photocopied.

Chapter 11. What Do They Really Want?
Cracking the Want Ad Riddle.

Bottom Feeders complain that the reading help wanted ads can be like trying to make sense out of Egyptian hieroglyphics. So they limit themselves to skimming the ad for the vitals such as: job description, wages and benefits offered and where the job is located. Unfortunately, this seriously limits the impact of the information they will include in their cover letter.

Learning to glean the critical information that the want ad offers to a job seeker is vital. One key piece of advice that career counselors and resource managers share with job seekers is to not shrink away from the opportunity. "You don't need to have everything they say, because they are looking for the ideal person," says Leslie Armistead, Information Services Manager at the Career Action Center, in Cupertino, California. "If you have two-thirds of what they are asking for, you've got a pretty good chance of making it past the first cut."

Intelligent employers' primary concern is to hire the best person for the position. Having all the 'right' credentials isn't necessarily an equation for guaranteed success.

Bottom Feeders will let educational requirements deter them from applying. Ideally, an employer would love to have someone with the exact education or degree, apply for the position. They are willing to take a look at a candidate that has the capability of performing to their expectations. If you don't have the education required in the ad, don't pass on the opportunity.

Take a moment to think of what the job entails. Does the education you have fit in any way? What are the similarities? This is where the power of your cover letter can make the difference. Describe how your education will benefit this position. Don't assume they will be able to make the connection. Tell them why your education or experience is a good fit. Managers and employers understand that someone with a proven track record for succeeding in the trenches or out in the field, could have a great deal more to offer than someone who only has an academic background.

Be bold and flaunt the skills you've picked up in the real world. Use your lack of the specific credential as a hook. "Book smart or street smart, which would probably be more successful for this position? For the past ten years, I've demonstrated my ability to lead and inspire employees, generate sales and keep operational costs to a minimum. This resulted in taking a small business and tripling the sales in a two-year period. I promise to bring the same level of commitment, drive and business savvy to your business." This is likely to have more impact than a piece of paper proclaiming that you made it through the course without quitting.

Another stumbling block can be the demand for X number of years experience. Keep in mind that the amount is not etched in stone. They are looking to see competency more than longevity. Show that what you have accomplished prepares you for whatever this position may face. Give an example of one of your successes using skills and abilities that you know are critical for success in this position. Remember that a required ten years of experience in management can be substituted with ten years combined experience in supervisory and positions of elevated responsibilities.

Some motivational speakers will encourage you to 'fake it, til you make it.' This will backfire on you if the skill you are trying to fake is a technical skill. Pretending I know how to write computer software programs or operate a piece of equipment I've never seen before will come to light very quickly in the interview. There is nothing to gain by embarrassing yourself and annoying the potential employer.

Dissecting a Help Wanted Ad.

There are two key areas to consider when analyzing the requirements of the ad: the announced requirements and assumed needs. Make two separate lists. In the first, list the requirements in the same order that they appeared in the ad. Often the order will suggest the importance of each item. On the second, list the needs that you believe would be important to the employer.

Example of a help wanted ad.

Legal Secretary, Remson, Baxter & Vivaldi Law office is seeking a Legal Secretary to fill a maternity leave vacancy on a part-time basis commencing January 6, 2003. The successful candidate will be organized, able to work independently, exercise initiative, and have a minimum of two years litigation experience. Please forward resumes to Vera M. Hoffman. # 206, 6002 – 10th Ave. Vancouver, BC V6Z 2P3 Email getoutofjail@law.ca

Employer's Noted Needs:

1. Minimum two years experience
2. Organized
3. Work independently
4. Show initiative

Employer's Assumed Needs:

1. Display confidentiality
2. Accurate and detail oriented
3. Speed and efficiency
4. Office skills

Employer's Need: Experienced Legal Secretary
Your Skills: Ten years experience in a busy law office

Employer's Need: Organized
Your Skills: Demonstrated effective organizational and time management skills while working in a three lawyer law office handling hundreds of clients.

Employer's Need: Worked Independently
Your Skills: Began as sole Legal Secretary, eventually supervising a staff of five administrative staff.

Employer's Need: Show initiative
Your Skills: Initiated and implemented Customer Appreciation Greeting Card campaign that resulted in a 15% increase in repeat business.

Assumed Need: Confidentiality
Your Skills: Worked on documents of extremely personal, sensitive and confidential nature.

Assumed Need: Accurate and detail oriented
Your Skills: Worked on legal documents where mistakes were unacceptable

Assumed Need: Speed and efficiency
Your Skills: Type 100 wpm

Assumed Need: Office skills
Your Skills: Supervised an administrative staff of five

Your top skills to mention in opening paragraph:

Example: Throughout my ten years experience as a Legal Secretary in a busy law office that served

Larry Arrance

                          hundreds   of   clients,   I
                          demonstrated my ability to do
                          highly   detailed   work   in   an
                          efficient,   effective,   and
                          confidential manner.

Utilize the middle paragraph to bring attention to other
announced and assumed needs not already mentioned.
Do not assume that everyone else applying for the
position have the same skills and experience. Paint a
picture of how you are ideal for the position, with
examples of where you succeeded in both categories.

Close your letter by requesting an interview:

Example: Please contact me at (250) 000-0000 to
                arrange an opportunity to discuss how I can
                best be of service to your business.

126

Chapter 12. Recruiting Your Army.

Oh no, not the "N" word! Has there been any term more overworked than this one? Why do people keep slapping job seekers upside the head with the word *networking*? Because of all the methods known for finding employment, nothing works as effectively as networking. Most of us associate networking with the endless stream of annoying soon to be ex-friends and acquaintances that were relentless sharing their "make millions ground floor opportunities with us. Annoying or not, the system works. Not only for moving products and services but especially for connecting you to an awesome job or career opportunity. You say you're not the networking type? Swoosh. That was the sound of a Shark gliding past as he swallows up that great job while you floundered around reading want ads and waiting for a job to fall into your lap. If you're not networking, you're missing out on over 85% of the job opportunities. Most, and probably the best jobs are never advertised.

Expand your base of operations. What makes you think you can or even try to do this huge undertaking all on your own? Wouldn't it make a lot more sense to have one hundred, one thousand, or more sets of eyes looking for great opportunities for you than just your two? They say the average person knows 250 people and guess what - those people know people. When you talk to a friend or relative, don't just see them as someone you know and care about, see them as a treasure chest of possible leads. Everyone you know is connected to other people. Tap into that connection. If you have lived in your community for even a short time, unless you've been like the ultimate Bottom Feeder and have stayed indoors guarding your television, you will have met people. Through your circle of friends and acquaintances, you should know literally thousands of people. Don't you think it's reasonable for at least one of them to know of a job opportunity for you?

Compile a list of everyone you know. Start with the names of your family. Yes, you probably will know a lot of the same people but you can be sure there will be some different ones too. Move onto your friends even the ones you'ren't too crazy about right now. When I say friends, they don't have to be tried and true, take a dying blood soaked vow of brotherhood kind of friend. People to whom you can say "Hi how ya doin?" will do. Unless it has been like a zillion years because you've been in school, (in which case you're too old to be working anyway), contact some of your old school mates. They say it isn't what you know but who you know that lands you the job. Yes, I know that isn't fair but so what? Do you think a Shark will care if they get the finest morsels to eat while the Bottom Feeders are swimming around below waiting for the scraps? No, and neither should you.

If I could offer you an opportunity where you only had two possible outcomes, you either win big or break even, would you take it? Well, it's called networking. Think about it. When you start talking to people, which is all that networking is, you will either come out ahead with good information, a contact, or you will walk away with exactly the same thing you had before the conversation. You can't lose. They can't take knowledge away from you. You can't lose a job. This is the safest proposition you will ever get. Is courage necessary? Absolutely but it is something that will grow every time you introduce yourself to someone.

"Oh yeah, you and whose army?" Do you remember that from when you were a kid? Well, I want you and your army to work as a unit to find and uncover terrific job lead information for your campaign. Your army consists of you, family and friends. Have them spread the word faster than an email virus that you're looking for work and the kind of work you want. Be organized. Have them create a list of whom they know and who could possibly help with your search. You're wondering why these people would go to all this trouble for you, right? The reason is simpler than you think. People like to help. Think about the last time you helped someone. Did you like the feeling? Well, give them the same opportunity to experience that good feeling. Another reason people are willing to pitch in and help is because there is a very good likelihood that they have experienced the same situation themselves and don't like it any more than you do.

"Okay, so I have my list of names together, what should I ask them?" If you're like a typical Bottom Feeder your thinking will be very limited. Many Bottom Feeders won't even ask this one simple question. "Do you have a job for someone with my skills and abilities?" Most Bottom Feeders are standing around waiting for an employer to say "Here is job, would you like it?" When you're out connecting with people, by all means ask that first question but don't get discouraged if you don't get a direct hit with it. The odds are not in your favor. You must move on to question number two "Do you know of anyone who could use someone with my kinds of skills and abilities?" This gets the person thinking outside of his or her own small world. If that doesn't bring about the desired results, move in with question number three. "Who do you know that knows a lot of people?" That is the person with whom you want to make contact. You can be pretty certain that amongst their circle of influence lies the contact that can give you what you want. The biggest reason people take so long to find employment is that they don't tap into their network beyond the first level, if that.

"Some of the people I know probably couldn't do me much good." That's what you're thinking isn't it? Don't be too hasty to prejudge whom they know and whom they don't. If you were that clairvoyant, you wouldn't be unemployed. Everybody, and I mean everybody, is a potential treasure trove of contacts. And there is only one way to find out - ask them. Remember, you can't lose anything by engaging them in a conversation. If they don't know anyone, fine, now you know for sure that they can't help. Besides they'll be good practice for your next person.

Get in the habit of asking the three questions to everyone you meet. You don't know who or what someone knows until you have a conversation with them. One of the exercises I have my class go through is to brainstorm reasons why a position might be coming available or has come available. The following is a list of some of answers that have come up, you may think of some others.

- Quit
- Transferred
- Expansion
- Retired
- Injured
- Vacation
- Illness
- Death
- New technology
- Promotion
- Demotion
- Stress
- Office politics
- Fired
- Relocated
- Married
- Divorced
- Seasonal
- Lottery
- Incarceration
- Back to school
- Merger
- New contract
- Government grant
- Maternity / Paternity
- Office romance

The point behind this exercise is to drive home that there always different situations and life events happening in any business. Think about your own life. How often does it stay the same for any length of time? Well, it's the same for everyone else out there. Every business, every team and every employee is experiencing life changes. And with changes comes opportunity.

Every company experiences attrition. Even good employees leave businesses. Don't make assumptions as to whether a company is currently hiring. A Shark automatically figures there will be turnover, especially if employers have a chance to acquire the Shark's skills and experience.

Bottom Feeders are great at making assumptions. Teen-aged girl told me she was looking for a part-time position. I'd had been talking with an employer and they told me that they were in the hiring mode. I passed on the information to her and recommended hustle and apply for a job. Later, I checked back with her to see how it had gone. She told me that when she went down to the store, she looked through the window. "They didn't look like they were hiring," she told me. It was then that I knew she had super vision and that it wasn't working very well. Learn from her mistake. If you want to know what is going on in a company, ask somebody. Remember that Sharks won't wait for a meal to come to them. They go to the meal.

Now that I have you all primed up and you're ready to go out and network, network, and network some more, where do you go? The family and friends thing is pretty simple. You go wherever they are. If they're going to help you, the least you can do is meet them on their turf. Networking among strangers and minor acquaintances shouldn't be a happenstance occurrence. Plan ahead of time to meet people and expand your circle of influence. Instead of focusing on working on your six pack or developing killer biceps, plan to talk to other gym goers or staff. Rather than pumping iron, pump for information. Same thing for your church, synagogue or mosque, anywhere where people gather is a networking opportunity. There are other great places to meet and greet people and develop great job leads. Depending on the size of the city that you live in, there will be meeting halls, convention centers and hotels that host large conferences or meetings. Contact them and find out what seminars, business shows or conventions are coming to town and find out how you can take advantage of them.

The reason that networking doesn't work for Bottom Feeders is because they forget the middle word "work". Yes, it is work. It takes energy but the payoffs are phenomenal. If a Bottom Feeder does make it to one of those functions, they can be spotted standing by the free nibblies or off by themselves in the corner. They might be better off staying at home. A Shark goes to the networking opportunity with an agenda. They know ahead of time what information they want, which person they want to meet and who needs to see them. Like the old saying "If you fail to plan, then you're planning to fail." It's amazing how the information you're looking for pops up in conversation when you're focused on finding it.

Where are you volunteering right now? If you aren't then you had better give it some serious consideration. Volunteering serves many different purposes. If you're new to an area, then find an organization that you believe in and volunteer your services. This will put a local name on your resume so that not all the information is from somewhere else. It also starts your local network of contacts. Employers have a soft spot for people who volunteer. It shows them that you're willing to give of yourself and that not everything you do is about money.

Volunteering can open up a lot of opportunities for you. Some people will volunteer for organizations to pick up skills they didn't have before. My first computer skills were acquired while I traded my services to a women's organization for time on their computers. One of my clients gained the skill of operating large television cameras and audio equipment while volunteering at a local cable programming facility. Would she have acquired those skills anywhere else for free? Another client volunteered at a party headquarters during one of the elections. After the election she had three job offers. Business people got the chance to see her in action.

Another client heard that many companies would allow volunteers to work for them as a safe way to assess whether they would make good employees. She contacted an agency that coordinates volunteers with opportunities. She had decided that she would give it her best try to demonstrate that she was a valuable asset. At the end of the first day, they approached her and offered her a full time position. They were not stupid. They recognized a good employee when they saw one. That is how a Shark operates. Everything is done with a purpose in mind. Many Bottom Feeders will volunteer but they forget why they are there. It is not to give away your time for free. Use the time to develop skills, develop contacts and to develop great letters of reference. A very wise man said that you should dig your well before you need it. The time to build a network is before you need one. The building of a network when you're feeling needy can make you uncomfortable because you may feel that you're doing all the taking and not giving anything back. If this is the case, don't worry about it. If you build a good network, the day will probably come when some of your network, will your help. What goes around comes around.

"I'm not much of a joiner." Lose that attitude in a hurry. You look at any successful person and they will have other successful people around them. There is no such thing as a self-made man, just ask his mother. You don't have to be in this thing alone and you shouldn't be. By joining organizations, you get the opportunity to tap into the circles of influence of movers and shakers. People who belong to organizations are, quite often, the leaders of companies, managers of departments or other dynamic individuals on the rise. How do I know this? Because they are doing non-Bottom Feeder things like sticking to themselves or sitting at home in front of the brain drain machine also known as the TV.

Dive into the middle of a pool of resources and contacts. Go where power and camaraderie can make a difference in your life. I'm a big believer in the power of positive association. That's why I belong to Toastmasters International. This is a worldwide organization that supports individuals in their development of communication skills. The reason I have been with them for over seven years is because I know that I can count on being surrounded by, and learning from, people who want more from their lives. As they strive and grow, guess what? I grow right along with them. Do yourself a favor and find an organization that shares your values and does work that you can support. Other benefits besides expanding your circle of influence exponentially is the opportunity to acquire skills you never had before by volunteering to serve in an executive role with the organization and creating a chance to build friendships.

Even though aligning yourself with successful people is a very Shark thing to do, don't worry about it seeming too mercenary. Most of the other in the organization will have joined for basically the same reason. Networking isn't just for job seekers. You won't be doing all the taking in this relationship. I'm pretty confident that you will have something of value for someone else in the organization. It could be skills that someone could utilize or maybe you have information that will prove beneficial to another member.

"Okay, so now that I've made contact with all these new people, what do I say to them when they ask me what I'm looking for?" A wise man once told me that *clarity* is power. The biggest obstacle facing a Bottom Feeder is lack of direction. They can't hunt down what they want because they don't have a clue what that is. Part of my job used to involve finding training placements for my clients. Naturally I wanted match up my people with training opportunities that were right for them. I would ask them what they would like me to get for them. Many would say "Oh I will take anything." In the beginning, I fell for that. I would go out and bring back an anything position. Wouldn't you know it? It was always the wrong anything. So I would take them by the hand and lead them to the window. I'd direct them to point to the anything so that I would know what I was looking for.

If you have ever heard jobseekers say, "Oh, I will take anything" (which by the way is the mantra of Bottom Feeders) tell them that there is an acid test for that statement. Ask them if they will flip burgers at McDonald's? (Not that there is anything wrong with McDonald's.) If the answer is no, then it's clear they won't take anything and we need some clarity. If you don't know what you're looking for, how can you expect anyone else to help you find it?

There is a simple clarification tool called the "Heaven and Hell" technique. Take out a piece of paper and make two lists. Under the heaven heading write, down all the things you want in a job. This could be working for a small company, working 9 – 5 Monday to Friday, dealing with people, doing teamwork, and being creative. The longer and more detailed the list the better. With each addition to the Heaven list, you're automatically eliminating occupations or jobs that don't have these things going for it. For a lot of people, focusing on all the things they want is too positive and pie in the sky. They prefer to come from the Hell end of things.

Have you ever had a job you didn't like? Great, write down all the things you didn't like about it. This will serve two purposes. One, it gives you a chance to bitch. Get it out of your system. Two, if you hate those things, then by flipping the items over and looking at whatever the opposite, you're eliminating the jobs that have those attributes. Most Bottom Feeders will not put this much effort into introspection. The result is very evident too because they wander in and out of wrong jobs and lousy working situations all their lives. Take the time and create some clarity. You're worth the time and effort.

"If I'm out talking to people, should I be handing out business cards?" There is nothing wrong with having business cards of your own. But in the world of networking it is actually more beneficial to receive business cards than it is to hand them out. Let's say that you and I meet. You give me your business card. How much control do you have that I will contact you? None, zippo and zilch. But, if I take your business card, how much control do I have that I will contact you? That's right, all of the control. So the power is in the hands of whoever is holding the business card. So why would you give the power away?

When you're with an employer or manager, ask for two business cards. One is to keep and the other is to give away. I'll tell them that I want an extra card in case I meet with someone who could do business with them. I'll write my name on the back before I give it away. Remember that networking is all about people helping people. Do you think they will have warm regards for me if someone ends up doing business with them because of me? You better believe it! On the other card, I'm going to wait until the earliest opportunity to jot down relevant information on the back of the card. Like it or not people are easy to forget. As soon as I'm out of eyesight, I'll record items on the back of the card regarding hair color, eye color, interesting personal things they mentioned. For instance, they may have talked about their kid being in a soccer tournament or that they were looking forward to their vacation. The next time I make contact with them, I'll ask how their kid did or how they enjoyed the vacation. They will be blown away that I remembered and cared enough to ask. I will have moved up from level one to level two.

Networking is about building relationships. Bottom Feeders seldom move up from level one. A Shark will constantly be looking for ways to create long lasting, mutually beneficial relationships. Business guru Harvey Mackay is the ultimate Shark when it comes to networking. His network of contacts is in the tens of thousands. When he needs something or a friend needs something, it's be an arm's reach away in his Rolodex. Start building a resource of contacts that can help you throughout your career.

The power of appreciation cannot be underestimated. People are more inclined to help you if they know their efforts were appreciated. Send a card or a letter or even take the time to drop it off in person. It will not go unnoticed. Consider the fact that they didn't have to do this for you and they didn't gain from the situation. A thank you of some kind can do wonders for their continued support. I was told of a woman who competed for a contract to do the landscape design for a large business project. She was nervous because she was going up against some very big competitors with very impressive track records. Amazingly, she was awarded the contract. She said it took two weeks to work up the nerve to ask why she was given the nod over the other competitors. They told her that of all the people that had bid on the job, she was the only one that sent a thank you note saying she appreciated the opportunity. They said they felt it was a classy thing to do and it impressed them.

Sales is a game of numbers. So is networking. They say that it takes on average 5 sales calls to make the sale. The less successful sales people will only make one sales call. And their paychecks reflect this mistake. The same can be said for job seekers. Do you really think you will impress anyone with just one visit? It takes many visits to develop a relationship. I have a friend who owns a restaurant. She says she gets young people coming in almost everyday to drop off a resume. She says she doesn't pay them much attention. It's the ones that come back three or four times that she'll take the time to talk to and give serious consideration. Anyone can walk around dropping off resumes. That doesn't show any real desire to work for her. When a person repeatedly comes back to ask for a position, she knows that person wants to work for her.

The beauty of you going in to see an employer on multiple occasions is that with each visit you become less of a stranger. When a position comes up, employers can choose between a candidate they have even a small relationship with or a stranger from the flood of resumes brought in from an ad in the paper. Put yourself in the employer's position. Do people lie on resumes? Absolutely. In actuality, men will lie three times as often as women on a resume. I believe it is because men are more creative and just need to express it more. The employer is faced with the prospect of sifting through a mountain of possible lies and exaggerations or taking a chance on someone who has shown drive, dedication and commitment in their pursuit of employment with him. Which option would you take if you were the employer?

If you're concerned that the employer will be annoyed and consider you to be a pest, then ask him. Tell them that you're serious about finding a position with them and that you would like to drop by from time to time to let them know that you were still interested. Then ask them how often would be appropriate without becoming a pest. One of my clients was trying to get on with the hospital. In his conversation with the head of the supplies department he asked how often was appropriate for popping in. The department, head told him to come in once a week because that way he would remember his face and be more likely to choose him when an opening came up. Honesty is always your best policy. Be straight with them and they are likely to be straight with you.

Not all networking involves actually meeting the people. Many people will take advantage of the huge volume of people on the Internet. You can join email mailing lists where information is emailed to you based upon a particular group's interest. Another option is to connect with a newsgroup or USENET. This takes a little more effort on your part because you have to tap into a bulletin board to read messages. You can read the information someone has posted and reply. Keep in mind that your reply will be posted. Other people can respond to either the original information or your posting. As an added benefit, many of these sites allow you to post your resume or contain job postings.

Chapter 13. Thirty Seconds and You're In!

Enlist the help of Alexander Graham Bell to save you time and money. That's right! Use the telephone to speed up your work search. Looking for work can eat up time and money so you must be Shark smart. A typical Bottom Feeder would rather risk jumping in their car or even hop on a bus and go to a business than use the telephone to make contact with the employer. This is both costly and stupid. You look at any good sales person. They will use that very effective tool called the telephone to set up appointments with a possible prospect.

It's efficient because you can concentrate your efforts and make the most of your time - especially if you're using the bus as transportation or don't own your own gas station. You can set up your interviews in clusters by geographical areas and reduce your traveling time. Now many clients are baffled at the mention of having so many interviews that you need to cluster them, when up to now they were lucky if they had one or two interviews a week. There has been a shift in the definition of an interview. For most of my clients, and especially the Bottom Feeders, an interview is when an employer invites you in, takes out the rubber hoses and bright lights and beats the information out of them. Michael Farr, in his book *The Very Quick Job Search*, best describes the new breed of interviews. The new definition of an interview is any face-to-face meeting with someone who can hire you or supervise you. This can be as short as a thirty-second conversation in the lobby of a business. That is an interview. As long as the two of you have had a meeting, consider it an interview.

By using the telephone you can set many such interviews throughout the day. This technique can generate two, three, four or more interviews per day. At that rate, you will have gone from two interviews per week to ten, twenty or more. Obviously, your odds for finding a job offer increase with the greater number of face-to-face meetings.

"Why would people want to meet you for all these meetings or mini interviews?" Remember that *greed gland* I mentioned earlier? Well, it's time to target it again. When you're using the phone to contact employers, the key is to give before you receive. Use a phone spiel, much like a telemarketer or phone sales person. To make contact with the employer, you have to give them a reason to want to meet you. I cringe when I overhear a Bottom Feeder who asks an employer on the phone that brutal question "are you hiring?" "Do you have any jobs open?" Why would an employer tell you even if they had an opening? Here is some faceless voice on the other end of the line, who could be anyone from a serial killer to the Uni-bomber. Talk about scaring an employer.

You need to give me a reason to meet you first. Keep this in your mind at all times: an employer will hire you for one reason, and only one reason, to make a profit. That may seem cold to you but that is the blunt truth. It won't be because they had an empty office or they had too much money in the bank and needed to share the wealth. You will be required to generate money, save money or create an environment where the employer can go out and create wealth. So basically, when you contact the employer you'll be telling them why you're likely to be doing one of those things for them.

Here's a sample telephone spiel. You'll want to have a spiel or script because it's better to be prepared with the information you need to get across than to wing it. Being prepared will sound more intelligent. Please feel free to alter it until it feels right for you.

"Hi my name is Randy Freedman. I have over 10 years experience in the logging industry. I can operate a full line of Timberjack, John Deere and Caterpillar line and grapple skidders, Caterpillar and Case bulldozers, John Deere and Caterpillar front-end loaders. I'm also very good at maintenance and repairing machinery. I'd like to have the opportunity to meet with you. When would be a good time for you?"

What the employer will be doing is mentally checking off all the items you have mentioned that are valuable to him. And you will notice that he did not ask for a job. You're likely to get yeses to a time to meet because there's no risk for the employer at all.

"Once I have my spiel ready, should I memorize it?" No, keep it written down and close by the telephone when you're calling. When you're nervous there is a better chance that you will forget something. It will probably sound a little wooden at first but that will go away quickly as your spiel becomes second nature to you. Don't be surprised when you get in to the natural rhythm of your spiel, it seems like they have their own script on the other end. All of their uh ha's and umms will be in the right spots as you lead them in for the close.

"Why do I have to go to all that bother? Couldn't I just call the personnel department?" There is a saying in the industry "You only go to the Personnel department when you want to work for the personnel department." The reason is that this department is always the last to hear about anything. Any manager or department head will know whether they need someone long before the personnel department, so it makes sense that you would go to them first.

My brother-in-law was applying for a position as a heavy-duty mechanic for a local mine. He approached the personnel department only to be told that there were no positions available. As he was leaving, he bumped into a man wearing coveralls. They got into a conversation. It turned out that this man was the foreman at the mine. He was happy to hear that my brother-in-law was a mechanic because they had needed one for a while now but hadn't found the time to get the message to the front office. My brother-in-law ended up working there for over ten years.

Personnel departments were invented to fill positions within the organization but have mutated into a very effective method for screening out Bottom Feeders. The only time a Shark has any contact with this department is when the manager or department head, that wants them hired, guides them through it. So make a point of targeting the person who has the power to hire you or supervise you. Go talk to a professional salesperson and ask them why they qualify their prospect. They know it's a waste of time to make a pitch to someone who doesn't have the authority to make the purchasing decision. Treat the sale of your product the same way.

"I have never been very good on the phone and I'm nervous about using it" Being nervous or afraid is normal. Feel the fear and do it anyway. The payoff is so huge that this step cannot be overlooked. Most people's length of unemployment is unnecessarily long because they don't have a system for coming up with job leads. It makes total sense that you're afraid because it's natural when doing something you haven't done before. Practice on friends and family until most of the nervousness has dissipated. This is a skill like any other, so consider yourself in training. If it will make you feel any less stressed, practice on businesses in which you're only mildly interested. That way if you don't get the positive response you were hoping for, it won't be much of a setback. The worse that can happen is they invite you in for an interview.

"What happens if when I do call them, they are not interested and they say no?" Persistence is key. You have a good product. You believe in your product. You know the product would be of benefit to their business. If you don't show a little resolve and don't stand up for your product, they may miss out on a very valuable employee and you both lose. Here is a sample conversation with an employer:

Receptionist answers – "Hello, may I speak with Mr./Ms. O'Sullivan?"
(Asking for them by first name can have more impact.)

Mr./ Mrs. O'Sullivan – "Hello"

You – "Mr./Ms. O'Sullivan – go into your telephone spiel." Ask for a time to meet.

Mr./ Mrs. O'Sullivan – "NO"

You – "Thank you, Mr./ Mrs. O'Sullivan, but I would like to have an opportunity to meet and discuss any future openings.

Mr./ Mrs. O'Sullivan – "Yes"

You – "Would 10 a.m. tomorrow be okay?"

Mr./ Mrs. O'Sullivan – "Yes"

OR

Mr./ Mrs. O'Sullivan – "NO"

You – "Thank you for your time anyway, Mr./ Mrs. O'Sullivan. Would you know of any other employers in your field who may have an opening?"

Mr./ Mrs. O'Sullivan – "Yes"

You – Ask name and "May I use your name as a referral?" "Thank you again, Mr. / Mrs. O'Sullivan, for your time. May I call back in a few weeks or so to keep up with the job situation?"

"Okay they said yes, what should I do now?" Above all, come across as professional. Show them that you're organized by asking them to confirm to specific time. There is more than one method. Some people prefer to give them a choice. "Do you prefer morning or afternoon? Which would be better for you?" Or be direct, "would tomorrow morning at 9 am be good for you?" It doesn't matter which you use, just as long as you get a specific time. If they tell you sometime next week would be fine, don't settle for that. Tell them that you're a very organized person and would prefer to write in a specific time to meet in your daytimer. Be gracious at all times and thank them again for the opportunity and their time.

When you're calling an employer, you want one of three things from the phone call. One, you want the face-to-face. Two, you want to get a better time to call in case you called at an inopportune time. Three, you want a referral.

"Why would the employer want to give me a referral?" The employer doesn't have a reason to fear giving you information about a possible lead with another employer. Quite often, they'll feel a little guilty that they couldn't help you out, especially if you have been polite and friendly throughout the conversation. The beauty of the referral is that the employer, who gives it to you, thinks it is a minor concession. Believe me it won't be minor to you. When you use the employer's name with the person they suggested, it can open the door very wide for you. Whatever positive feelings the new contact has for the person who referred you; it will be automatically attached to you. I was always amazed at the great treatment I received from someone after I mentioned that one of their peers recommended that I contact them. When a good salesperson (a.k.a. Shark) makes a sale, before the money has even changed hands, they will be asking for referrals. They know that by using the name of the first buyer the others are already more than half sold.

"What happens when I run into the receptionist?" Remember why she is there and the job she is supposed to be doing. Part of her job could be to screen out unnecessary calls from reaching and possibly irritating her boss. Please keep in mind that yours is a very necessary call because that business needs your services. Be friendly, bright and upbeat. There is a pretty good chance the receptionist has dealt with difficult or moody people already that day. You can be a pleasant surprise. If the receptionist comes across as open and friendly, then by all means try to develop some rapport with her. The only real hazard with this can be if you're somehow competing for her job.

Don't expect a good deal of support from the receptionist. If she is approachable, then be direct. Tell her why you're phoning and quickly list what you have to offer the employer. It can never hurt to have an ally within the company. But keep in mind that because she is the receptionist, she may be unlikely to know if a certain department head or manager is hiring or in need of someone. Your best bet is to connect with the person with the power.

Another way to get beyond the receptionist/watchdog is to use psychology. When you phone in and ask for the person you want by name. She is likely to challenge you but not always. I was astonished, when I used to phone employers, how often I was patched immediately through to the head of the business. The receptionist may ask you what the call regards to. Your answer: "It's personal." The receptionist is not likely to challenge you or probe further because she doesn't need to pry into the private affairs of her employer. And you're not lying because what is more personal than the work that you do?

"Will an employer leave a message on an answering machine?" An employer will need to reach you and you cannot always be home. Most employers will not have a problem leaving a short message for you on your machine unless they are trying to fill a warm body position. In that case, they are more or less looking for the first live person who can show up for the next shift. When you put your message on a machine, keep in mind that even your message is part of your sales pitch. I have a friend that thought it would be funny to have the voice of Fran Drescher's Nanny as his message. Unfortunately for him, I found it too irritating to listen to. I could never last long enough to leave him a message. If he was using it as a message eliminating device, then it was a smart recording. Otherwise, he wasn't getting the full value from his answering machine.

I don't care if your five-year-old child is adorable. That's not who should be leaving the message. When an employer phones, your message will be telling them something about you. Having a cutesy, cuddly message from your children may raise concerns about childcare or other child related issues. You could be eliminated before ever getting the chance to sell yourself. If you think that they will decide you're creative or fun loving with your kooky, bizarre message, you're probably wrong. Their concern will be that you may be unprofessional with their business too. I heard about a Bottom Feeder that thought it would be hilarious to leave this message "This means we are not at home and most likely out buying beer or trying to score some dope!" It's pretty clear who the employer will think is a dope.

Keep your message short and simple. Give your last name. Tell them that you're away from the telephone right now but will respond as soon as possible. Thank them for leaving a message. Keep it personable and professional. Save the crazy stuff for when you're with your friends.

"What if I don't have an answering machine is it okay to use a pager or a cell phone?" Cell phones are acceptable but if you do receive a call, ask if you can call them right back on a land line so that there isn't a chance of a poor reception. As for a pager, don't bother. Find someone or some place that will let you use their phone as a message line. One employer told me that he figured anyone with a pager as the only source of contact was either a drug dealer or a hooker. It also doesn't create an image of stability, reliability or responsibility.

"What if they ask me to come in and fill out an application?" Are you really any further ahead? Not really, you probably could have gone down there on your own and filled out an application. Remember you want the face-to-face. Tell them "I would be happy to do that Mr./ Ms O'Sullivan. I believe I have a great deal to offer your company and I would love the opportunity to work for you when there is an opening. Would it be possible to see you when I've completed the application form? When would be the best time for me to do that?"

"Oh no! What if they want to interview me right then and there on the phone?" Like a Boy Scout, be prepared. Keep all your material near the phone. This is your command centre. It is important to have your resume, references and any certificates in one spot in case you need to refer to them. This is especially important if you lied on your resume and need to keep the facts straight! Most professional sales people will keep a mirror in front of them when they speak on the phone. No, it is not because they are so incredibly vain they can't stand to be away from their sweetheart for too long. It's because it has been proven that you can hear a smile over the phone. Smiling changes the physiology of your face, mouth and throat. The smile causes your voice to be warmer and more fluid and is more appealing to the ear.

Chapter 14. Discover Where Most of the Jobs are Hiding.

According to an industry survey this is how most jobs are found:

66% through personal contacts

15 % through a search firm

9% through classified ads

8% through blind mailings

Before you carve these figures in stone, you should know that 70% of all statistics are made up as they are needed. But for now, we will approach this chapter as if the figures were gospel.

We had a client that came into our office dressed in camouflage battle fatigues. We could only assume he was dressed to go after the "hidden job market." My guess after looking at this embarrassment to the other Bottom Feeders was that if he does go out looking for employment, the hidden job market would want to stay hidden. You've probably heard the term hidden job market many times but by now you have a pretty good idea that the jobs are not really hidden. Most of the unadvertised jobs are merely put out of reach where the Bottom Feeders rarely look. Employers want to fill all their positions but they don't want just anybody coming by their business.

Remember back in the chapter on networking, the statistics show that as much as 80 – 90% of positions are filled without posting a job ad.

"Does this mean I shouldn't bother with want ads?" Oh, by all means go through the want ads. They are a source of job leads and should be utilized. Just don't make them your only source. Immediately respond to any ad that intrigues you. If you have the luxury of tailoring your resume to that position – wonderful. If not, then craft your cover letter to the requirements of the position. Some people have suggested that you shouldn't be too hasty to get your resume in too soon. They are concerned that its like contestants that go first in a competition, they tend to be used as a benchmark and are unfairly judged. I don't believe it myself. My belief is that if you write a powerful sales-pitch demonstrating what you have to offer, it won't matter when its received

I created a resume and cover letter for a client and we submitted it the moment we saw the ad. She was contacted within the hour. After she had won the position, she was told that it was the best cover letter and resume they had ever received. This was an international company with thousands of employees. She was also told that hers was the first resume received for that position and it was used as the benchmark. The difference was that they wanted to see if any resume could reach her standard.

Don't worry about when you send the resume in; just make sure it is the best one for the position. If an ad looks like the job is going to attract a lot of attention, you might want to consider sending in another resume for the position after about one week. The first one may have got caught up in the tidal wave of resumes and overlooked. Just explain in your cover letter that your interest in the position was so great that you resubmitted to demonstrate you genuine desire to work for them.

"How long is an ad good for?" There is no official time limit for an ad, so don't hesitate to send in your resume. What we recommend people do is to go back through the archives of newspapers want ads for the last three months. If you find a job advertised that you would have applied to it, had you seen it, then go ahead and apply to it. Naturally, if it is a post office box ad, the post office box will have long because been reassigned and it will be a cold trail to follow. Why would I want you to go after old newspaper ads? What is the normal probation period for a job? Three months is typical. Maybe Joe or Jane isn't working out but they haven't replaced them yet. This technique can eliminate the competition because you're the only one applying for the position.

Obviously, you don't mention that you just noticed their ad from two months ago and are just sending in a resume now. Send your cover letter as a simple prospecting tool telling them what you have to offer the firm. One of my clients was surprised when he used this method. The company was still happy with the person they had hired but the employer had two other positions that were coming available. He managed to snag one of them before it was ever advertised.

"But if some companies do post ads and can get decent employers, why don't they'll post ads?" Some companies are terrified that if they post want ads they will be like the Statue of Liberty. *"Give me your tired, your poor. Your huddled masses yearning to breathe free. The wretched refuse of your teeming shore. Send these, the homeless, tempest-tossed to me."* Unfortunately for employers, the vast majority of job seekers that apply for a position are hopelessly unqualified. Sifting through the unqualified applicants is costly in both time and money. This is why some employers would gladly pay for a head hunting company to find qualified people. It's cheaper in long run. Also, for most companies, it isn't necessary to post ads because the Sharks have uncovered the leads and eaten up the opportunities.

One of the most common laments I get from Bottom Feeders is that there isn't some kind of state-run employment agency that hands out jobs. They'd like it if someone would just send them to a business and the job was automatically theirs. I ask them why would they want to give that much control of their lives to someone else. Would they want someone else to go out and pick their next mate? Mind you, looking at most Bottom Feeders, perhaps it might not be such a bad idea. I can't imagine when I would be better off having some stranger tell me where I will be working and what I will be doing without my input on the subject. Agencies that used to do that were an abomination. They crippled many people by treating them like small helpless children. It's like the old saying "Feed a man a fish and you feed him for a day.

Teach him how to fish and you feed him for a lifetime." These people should have been trained to be self-sufficient and find employment on their own.

"Okay already, I get your point. How do I know which company to call?" If you're like most job seekers, you won't have a definite list of potential employers to go after each day. We are going to correct that problem. There is a very simple, yet effective, way to generate job leads. Take out your local phonebook. Go to the index section. Start at the beginning. Look at each listing and ask yourself, "Could they use somebody with my skills?" Do not limit yourself. Think of the entire business. When I ask my class how many of them are targeting high-tech companies, very few hands will go up. I then ask them why they weren't. Most just stare back at me blankly or say, "because I don't do high-tech stuff." They have made the same wrong assumption that most Bottom Feeders make - that high-tech companies only have high-tech jobs. Again, think about the entire company. They have technical jobs, administration jobs, sales jobs, shipping and receiving jobs, etc. It's the same with most businesses. There are lots of different areas in the business - all requiring different skills. How can you fit into that company?

Go through each listing and consider all the different areas they may have. Could they use your skills even in an entry-level position? Let's take, for example, someone with customer service or clerical skills. Do most businesses have positions where having great customer service skills or perhaps an administrative

159

background would be valued? Of course they do! If the answer is yes and they could use someone with my skills, I would check them off and move down the list. I have seen students generate forty, fifty or more categories. Some of my students asked me what to do with the categories of jobs that they would definitely not want to do. Easy. Don't check it off.

Their next step is to look at the index where they've checked and then go to section of the yellow pages indicated. That one checkmark could turn into many different businesses, depending on how large your city is. I have seen this exercise create a list of hundreds of possibilities. The value of this exercise is that you now have a list of possible targets instead of waiting for the opportunities to fall from heaven.

Remember what was said about approaching the personnel department. So focus your attention on the person or people who could use your skills. There are several ways of coming up with the appropriate person's name. You can research the company on the Internet and see if they give the name of the manager or department head. Another method is to go to the company and see if they have the business cards of the managers on the front counter. Wait outside the business and talk to someone who works there or phone the office and ask for the person's name, correct spelling and pronunciation.

If you do decide on an up-front and personal approach of just going to a business unannounced, go dressed like you were heading into the interview. When they said you only get one shot at first impression they weren't kidding. As a career coach, I've seen some very bizarre outfits worn by people who were supposedly looking for work. I thought the guy in the battle fatigues was the most ridiculous until one of my female clients showed up in her tiny lime green bikini and transparent beach cover up. I guess she wanted to make sure she made an impression. For a while I hung a mirror in the classroom with a sign underneath that read, "Would you hire this person?"

"How do I know if an employer needs me?" Turnover happens in every company. Our office is one of the greatest places to work and yet, we still have employees that move on. An intelligent employer will always have their eyes and ears open for a highly qualified employee that can be an asset to their firm. I have ex-managers or owners in my classes and they said that when people would drop in and see them, and if they were impressed with them, they would hang on to the resumes. Sometimes they would still give that person a call, even two years later, on the chance that that person might be available.

Staff challenges come up for every company and it is to their benefit to have an idea of what the replacement market for key employees is like in their area. An employer cannot hire you if they don't know you exist.

"What about going to companies that hand out job applications?" Some companies will only let you in through this process unless you've networked your way in. The application can be a simple one-page form, right up to an eight-page form like one of the major department store chains use. Others will have you fill in an application on-line through their website. My advice to you is if they let you leave with the application form, get it photocopied immediately. Work out all your answers on the practice sheet before transferring in to the final copy. Take your time and think your way through each question. If it is an on-line application, really take your time. Remember that the application is an excellent tool for screening you out. Don't give them any help doing that.

"Should I look at civil servant jobs?" Only if you have given up on finding an honest job. Just kidding!!! The civil service is faced with a lot of the same challenges that most companies are facing. Technology and attrition will take its toll on them, too. Even though it looks like many different levels of government are laying off lots of people, that doesn't mean they don't need someone with your skills? Just because a government is trying to be fiscally prudent by trimming down what they think are redundant or unnecessary positions doesn't mean that the work is no longer there. They may not be filling union ranks but may be considering someone doing the work under contract basis.

"Should I try union halls even though I'm not a member?" Sometimes they are the only route into a business. We have wineries in our area that will only hire through the union hall. They will obviously place members with the most seniority first before considering you. But if they have a position to fill it doesn't makes sense for them not to fill it because it means no one is working at the business and making their union dues contribution. Many unions will add to their ranks by bringing people on in entry-level positions. Your hours are likely to be on call, casual, part-time or seasonal. As your seniority builds, you will get more hours. Sometimes you can slip into union positions through connections. Do you think is by sheer coincidence that there are complete families working in the same union?

"My city offers government sponsored employment agencies. Are they really any help at all?" I can't speak for all of them but I would imagine that you'd be pleasantly surprised at the amount of help or assistance they can provide. This could be in the form of classes designed to help you develop job search skills, advice from counselors or training programs. The benefit of attending classes is the opportunity to network. Even though the room is full of unemployed people, it doesn't mean that one of them doesn't know of a position that would be right for you. You'll also find strength of community because you will understand that you're not alone going through this. There are others experiencing the same trials and tribulations. You can learn how they are handling the pressures and possibly apply it to your own life. The lessons you learn in class may be more powerful than reading it in a book. If you're the type of person who is more of a kinesthetic learner, you need to be in some kind of group interaction or role-play for this information to really sink in.

Larry Arrance

Employment counselors can provide some excellent guidance to someone on a career change path. Just be sure that they are actually listening to you and don't have some preconceived notions as to what you should become. Also check their credentials. I have met several so-called professional counselors who fell into the position by chance. Their advice has been, on many occasions, harmful, disastrous and expensive for the poor slob that believed them. One alleged professional had read an article about the up and coming jobs of the new millennium and made a mission of directing everyone into the computer industry. For one thing, there is no such thing as "the ideal job for the new millennium." There are very valuable skill sets to acquire that can be marketed for a long time but that doesn't mean they would be ideal for everybody. You have to do some investigation into your likes and dislikes, natural skills and abilities, and what you want to do with the rest of your life. If they match up with the so-called ideal jobs, great. If they don't that's okay too. There will be a need for what you're good at. Its just that you probably won't find it mentioned in some trivial article a so-called expert posted on the Internet.

Many agencies offer programs sponsored by the government that are designed to enhance your marketable skills through training and education or make you more desirable to employers by offering wage subsidy. Do not be embarrassed about accepting this kind of help. A Shark never turns down assistance that can benefit him or her. My only caution would be that, when you're out marketing yourself to employers, don't sell the subsidy first. The subsidy is icing on the cake. It should be used to give you an edge over the next applicant. When you market the subsidy first, you run the risk that the employer will think that your product is damaged and that the money is to make up for it. Many employers told me that they are turned off when an applicant walks in with a flyer saying that the government will pay the company thousands of dollars to take on this person. Their immediate reaction is to wonder why, what's wrong with this person? So sell your product as a stand-alone product that is worth full price just like all the rest. When they have hired you or thinking about it, then sell the benefits of the program, just to sweeten the deal.

"Should I place an ad in the paper?" Any method can work. This one doesn't have the greatest reputation for success but I have seen it work. You may have seen an ad posted in the Financial Post of Toronto, Canada. The headline read "Former Marijuana Smuggler." He went on to sell the experience he gained prior to going to prison. It was hugely successful. It was creative. He focused on the skills he had demonstrated in management and problem solving abilities he had demonstrated as a criminal. He took responsibility for his mistakes and sold the lessons he had learned. In other words, he took his material and packaged it so that an employer would focus on his good points and forgive the rest.

I wrote up an ad for a client. Because of her meager financial situation she was limited to twenty-five words. It was a tricky assignment but I managed. The result was eight employers responding to the ad. Unless you have a healthy bank account to draw upon for your advertising you had better make sure your ad is well-crafted. Focus only on the benefits that you will bring to the employer. Keep your words positive and action or results oriented. Do not be afraid to boast about your ability. Shy doesn't sell.

Chapter 15. Utilize the Ultimate Weapon for Getting Past Barriers.

Clarity is power. There, I've said it again. Be clear on what the company does and where they are headed. To know this gives you a great advantage when it comes to selling yourself. I remember when I was out looking for work in a totally Bottom Feeder state of mind. I was merely answering ads whether I thought I could do the job or not. I was using the "throw the spaghetti against the wall and see if any sticks" way of thinking. Against all odds, I received a call for an interview. At the interview I was asked what I could do for the company. In a moment of sheer Bottom Feeder brilliance, I asked them "What is it that you people do here?" Can you believe it? They didn't offer me the job!

Knowledge about the company will let you know where their weaknesses are and provide a possible way into the company. The more you know about a company the better you can see how you would fit into the business. Every company has problems. How can you solve even one of them? Can you increase sales? Can you develop new products? Can you help them retain customers? Can you show them how to cut costs? Treat this much like a military campaign. Get as much intelligence about your target before you make your move because to go in unprepared can kill any opportunity to win a position with them.

Like I said earlier, every business has problems. Doing research can uncover where the problems are and help you figure out how you can fix it for them. Sharks are problem solvers while Bottom Feeders are generally considered problems. So when you research a business, think in terms of what you could do for them.

Just because you can be good for the company doesn't mean it will be good for you. Look for things like how closely does the mission statement or values match up with yours? Does the corporate culture appeal to you? Is the working environment very formal or is it like a family. Is there a dress code? Is it flexible or will you be wearing a three-piece suit everyday? What kind of history do they have concerning human rights? Keep in mind that you're trading part of your life for this position and you will not get that time back when you're done. So making the right choice is very important. Most of us have had working experiences that were not worth the trade we made.

"What am I looking for when I research a company?" First of all, you want to see if the company has a future and if there is potentially any place in it for you. You want to look at their financial status, hiring practices, future developments, company stability, mission and values. It's right about now that the Bottom Feeders start to whine because they prefer the path of least resistance. Sharks know that the more work they do in the beginning of job search, the easier it is to capture the position. Here are the basic steps to research a company:

Step 1. Visit the company's website. Nowadays, most companies, medium or large, will have a website. The site can be a gold mine of information. Quite often they will divulge information about their history, financial status or annual report, mission and/or values, hiring or career opportunities, future plans, and products or services. Unfortunately, there are still a large number of smaller businesses that have not gone on-line.

Step 2. Call or visit the company personally. Many companies have literature concerning what they do and who their customers are. This typically comes in the form of Annual reports, Press kits, brochures, price lists, other promotional material and publications.

Step 3. Go on the Internet and tap into websites dedicated to compiling information about businesses. Canadians check out The Blue Book of Canadian Business, Canadian Business & Current Affairs (CBCA) Business, ComputerSelect Web. American sources are American Society of Association Executives, Yahoo! Professional Organizations, Yahoo! Company Directories, Fast Company, and Companies Online. The list is too exhaustive to go on. Do a search with your favorite search engine.

Step 4. Go to the library. Many of the larger libraries will have a person dedicated to knowing how to research a firm and what articles are available and where to find them. Make use of their knowledge.

Step 5. Go to your local Chamber of Commerce.
See what brochures or promotional materials they have
on your target company.

Step 6. Do informational interviews. Go right to the
source and ask them questions. This approach is more
appropriate to people changing careers or just entering
a field.

**Step 7. Keep up to date on the industry or
company in which you're interested.** Read about
recent developments in the newspapers or industry
magazines.

Step 8. Utilize your network. Talk to people and
find out the names of people who work at the business.
Make contact and get information you're not likely to
find on a website or in a brochure.

**Step 9. Become very familiar with their product
line or services**.   What products do they carry,
promote or use?   What stores or outlets carry their
products?   Talk to sales representatives in these
businesses and find out which products sell well and
which ones don't.

Longevity of the company is important unless you
enjoy this process of constantly finding a new position.
What are the industry trends and areas of growth? Is
this industry going through explosive growth or is it
being eroded away?   Are they staying ahead of the
curve by developing new products or services?   Do
they have a firm grip on their niche or is it under

constant attack by competitors? How long have they been in business? If they are a publicly traded company, what has their stock been doing for the last year? Is it growing steadily or experiencing massive spikes in both directions. Who is your target company's leading competitors? What are they up to and how will it affect this company?

Like a good street fighter, can the company roll with the punches? Will it be affected by new technologies and what steps are they taking to incorporate new technology? If there is a technological change, how will your position be affected? You're looking for a company that provides or encourages on-going training. They have a saying in the training industry "The only thing worse than training someone and losing them is not training someone and keeping them." Some of the most successful businesses will dedicate money to keeping their employees up-to-date with their skills.

In a recent study of 153 large and medium sized organizations by the Conference Board of Canada, they concluded "There is a definite relationship between executive development, better leaders and more effective, more profitable organizations. In spite of this relationship, it is surprising that of the largest Canadian organizations surveyed, only 40 per cent have a formal executive development policy or strategy."

Some companies still don't get it even though another Conference Board of Canada study demonstrated a positive correlation between investment in training and profitability. It is imperative that the company you're looking at has a positive attitude about training their employees. If they don't, they will need to resort to replacing employees with people possessing the newer and more in demand skills. It will be that or go out of business. If you haven't noticed, your well-being does not enter into the equation.

Your job will change, the markets will change, and the technology will change. Does the business have a history of being adaptable? Does it run heavy with overhead or is it a lean, mean business machine? One isn't necessarily better than the other.

Is the company publicly held or is it under private ownership? Is the management local or is at the mercy of a faceless board of directors? Can you get hold of an annual report? If you do not know how to read or interpret the material, connect with someone who can. Is the company a likely target for takeovers or mergers? If it is, how will this affect your position? Is the company under any pressure to slim down on its personnel?

When you're deciding if a company or industry will be a good fit for you figure out ahead of time what you're looking for in a company or industry. Do you want a dynamic and innovative company that lives on the cutting edge and specializes in whatever the trends demand or would you prefer a niche business that focuses on doing one thing very well or perhaps an industry that has roots that go back many decades and is solid and staid? Many people became millionaires riding the wave of popularity of the Dot.com companies and taking the risks that went with it. Many others in the same industry also found that the wave could crash as quickly as it swelled. People who chose the calmer waters of the blue chip companies mostly fared better because the companies rode the waves better. The downside of the tried and true is that you're unlikely to get rich quickly.

Now change the focus of your research to see how good the match will be between you and the company. What qualities does the company seek in an employee? For example, does it seek self-motivation, creativity, accuracy, customer service skills, or risk takers? What is the atmosphere of the everyday work place? Is it relaxed and team oriented or is it something out of a Dilbert cartoon? Do they focus on the tried and true or do they encourage innovation?

What are the company's hiring practices and procedures? Do they hire frequently? Do they advertise positions or do they only hire through referrals? Does the company prefer a resume or curriculum vitae? Do you have to fill out an application form in person or is it done over the Internet? Do you need to submit a cover letter with your resume? Remember, while you're getting all this information to get the name of whomever you're sending your marketing materials.

"How do I know if the information is correct?" The same way you would verify that any information about anything is correct. Go to several sources. Do not rely only on their website because companies are going to be seriously biased towards showing their good side. Decide first if the source is credible. If it is government sponsored, it is unlikely to be prejudiced towards any particular business. If you picked up information through a bulletin board or chat room, take into consideration that the person may have an axe to grind and is feeding out bogus or harmful information.

"How much time should I spend researching companies?" Good question. You don't want to be a victim of paralysis by analysis. It would depend on several factors - the size of the company, the position you were going after and the resources you have available. For a smaller company, your research could be limited to talking to employees of the company or informational interviews with management. The time investment goes up from there. Keep the bulk of your research time on the Internet to the evenings and leave your days open to network and do informational interviews. Too many Bottom Feeders find that hiding in front of their computer screens is an excellent way to avoid talking to people. Successful job searches require taking action, taking chances and getting interviews.

"Now that my head is crammed full of all this information, what do I do with it?" If you have come to the conclusion that this is a good opportunity for you, you had better get to work packaging your material for the sales pitch. Because you now know what the company stands for, where they are going and how you're likely to be a benefit to them, it's time put it into action. Your cover letter can now be targeted, by focusing on how you're a solution to their problem. Explain how similar your core values and your mission in life run parallel to theirs. Craft your resume or curriculum vitae to show you have the types of skills and training that they find important.

Larry Arrance

Chapter 16. Surf's Up!

Have you ever found a tool that was the answer to all your repair or building problems? No? And you never will. I get a good chuckle out of the people that come into my office thinking that if they only knew how to access and surf the web they would find a job right away. The Internet is a tool and that is all. It's a source of information and possible leads. Period. As to how great a tool it will be for you, depends on what you're using it for. If you're searching out positions that are what I would call on the lower end of the skill or demand spectrum such as food servers or janitors (not that there is anything wrong with these positions), the Internet will hold very little value for you. The companies that could use your services rarely advertise those positions on the Internet. If they post them at all, it would be on government-sponsored sites and your search will be done very quickly. If you're willing to relocate or if your skills are in demand then the Internet becomes a much better tool.

I had one client that would come into the Internet lab (fancy way of saying a small room with several of computers linked to the Internet). She would spend two to three hours per day doing searches to find out if there were any sales clerks positions at a local Revy Home & Garden Centre. I think it is important at this point to mention that the business itself was less than one block away. She would have been much better off just walking over there and talking to them. Don't use the Internet as a method for avoiding contact with an employer.

They don't call the Internet the Information Highway for nothing. That's what it was designed to do, deliver information. Use it to search out job leads, names of businesses or the people you need to make contact with. Most of the people I've seen using the Internet will go to the job listings sites and browse through the posted ads. They will focus on any job that directly relates to the desired position. That makes sense but, unfortunately, they stop there. They make the typical Bottom Feeder mistake of believing if they don't see what they want, then it must not exist. Sharks gets excited when there is blood in the water because they know that where's there is blood there is a meal. A Shark job seeker knows that if there is a job listing then there is a company that is hiring.

A job posting is a company's way of saying there is turnover happening. Use the job ad as an invitation to come in and check the company out. The job posting may not be what you're looking for but that doesn't mean there aren't positions there that are more to your liking. Many of the sites will display the job posting and the company that posted it. A Shark will follow the lead back to company and check them out. Often there will be a link back into the company's home page. Browse around, check them out, and decide if they are a company you would like to be involved with. You can find out about their values or mission statement and judge for yourself how closely they match yours. Another option, once you're inside the company's website, is to take a look in their career opportunities link. You may find something closer to what you're looking for. Another thing to do is to see where there offices are located.

The jobs posted will tell you where they are located. You will be able to tell if they are regional, national or international. If you're willing to move then it won't matter where they are posted. If you're not willing to relocate then see if they have offices in your state or province. Most Bottom Feeders stop looking if they don't post a job in their backyard. A Shark is smart enough to realize that just because they didn't advertise in their city doesn't mean they don't need someone in their city.

My wife works for a large international company with its head office in the US. They have a Canadian arm of the business with its head office in eastern Canada. She is attached to a branch office on the west coast of Canada. But she lives and works several hours away in another part of the province. So if you looked at a posting on the Internet, it would tell you that the position was in Vancouver because that's where the office is. If you were not willing to work in Vancouver, you would walk away from the opportunity. DON'T MAKE ASSUMPTIONS.

I was working with one of my clients. She told me she was looking for a sales position, something with challenge and potential. I told her about a large international company that offered consulting services to businesses throughout North America. We researched them on the Internet. She liked what she saw. When she went to the job opportunities link, it displayed that the only sales position they had open was in Timmins, Ontario. She immediately said that she wasn't interested in moving to Timmins for this job. If you're from Timmins don't take it personally.

I said, "Who said you did? The reason for looking up the company was to have you research them and see if they were the type of business you wanted to join. Contact them and talk to them." She followed my advice and contacted them through the contact information on their website. They seemed quite interested in her from their initial conversation and then she said that the problem was that they only had a sales opening in Timmins and that didn't work for her. They asked her where she was calling, from. She told them she was calling from the Okanagan Valley in British Columbia. The caller said that was great because they actually needed someone for that area. The final result from the phone call and steps the client took after that was that she ended up being the sales representative for her area. Just because they don't have an office in your city doesn't mean they don't need someone for your area. Nowadays, many people work from home. You could be one of them.

There is a site on the Internet called Workopolis. They have a quick job search section that breaks the search down into four categories. *Location, Keyword Search, Date and Now Hiring*. It is the *Now Hiring* that can be very interesting. Naturally, the only companies in this section are companies that are using Workopolis as a posting site. They will list the businesses in alphabetical order. Start with A and investigate the businesses. For instance, it will tell you that Coca Cola has 32 positions available. Now you have probably heard of Coca Cola before (unless you have been inside a cave because birth) but you may never have thought of approaching them for a job. What you're also likely to run into are companies or recruiting firms that you may never have heard of. The point being that it would be impossible to apply to a company if you did not know they existed.

The largest number of people who do find work as a result of the Internet are Sharks that find out the names of companies, research the names of the contact persons and let them know what they have to offer. They approach the old fashioned away, with cover letters, resumes or informational interviews. They don't use just one tool but their whole toolbox. So remember there is often more to a company than the single job posting.

"There seem to be so many job posting sites out there. Are some sites better than others?" Just like anything else, some things are more valuable than others. Many of the larger sites may be approached by the bigger firms but don't ignore any of them. A lead is a lead is a lead! Some of my favorites are workopolis.com, monster.com, flipdog.com and getajobyoufreak.com. The number of job posting sites grows daily and can be overwhelming. I recommend that you limit your Internet research and job search to the evening hours if possible. Your days would be better spent doing informational interviews and contacting employers.

"Do you have to really computer savvy to utilize the Internet?" No, but as a Shark you're going to make acquiring computer skills a critical step to your future. Okay, I won't lecture anymore about acquiring skills unless you force me. When I'm teaching my Internet Work Search class, the only requirement I have is that you have a basic understanding of the mouse. The Internet is a fairly easy tool to use. Too easy, sometimes, which is why so many parents are complaining about how much trouble Jr. can get into without much effort.

What I recommend before you log onto the Internet is that you know what you're looking for because the amount of distractions is incredible and an hour of your time can be swallowed up very quickly. Write it down; be specific about what you hope your search will turn up. Warning, if something is flashing and looks enticing, just ignore it. No, you have not won something. Does it seem likely that you won a contest that you didn't enter? KEEP FOCUSED. Determine if it is job leads, research on particular companies or career advice you're seeking before you log on. This will keep your search targeted and more likely to turn up sites related to what you need and not a place where someone is trying to sell you something.

To get extra information, connect with chat lines and bulletin boards. A starting point for finding an appropriate chat line or bulletin board using the yahoo.com or about.com directories. Many professional organizations will have chat lines that you can join. This can open up a dialogue with people in the industry that you're researching. As in anything, don't automatically accept everything you hear. Somebody may have an axe to grind with that particular company and not be totally honest with you. Unfortunately, with chat lines you're not dealing face to face with someone. Because the other person is operating from a position of anonymity they don't always act with integrity. So - reader beware. Warnings aside, the chat lines can be a great way to network and develop contacts.

"Are there ways to speed up my search so that I'm not sifting through piles of unrelated sites?" Tips for making your search more efficient can be found at the search engines home page. Do yourself a favor and see what their experts have to say. The simplest method to speed up your search is to know what keywords will generate the best results. When I'm instructing a class on Internet Work Search techniques, I try to establish a main condition for employment. If people are only looking for a particular job or will only work in a specified area, then that becomes their keyword. If they aren't willing to work outside their particular city then it is a waste of time to be checking out employment opportunities for an occupation in any other region. If restricted to a certain area, then consider using not just the city's name but perhaps the general area's name too. For instance, instead of doing a search for Kelowna, which is the name of a city, you could also do a search on the Okanagan, which is the region in which Kelowna exists. The number of postings the original search missed may surprise you.

"Why do I need to do all this work. Can't I just post my resume on those sites and let the employer come to me?" The commercial on TV that shows hordes of companies competing for the services of an employee by sending gifts and fruit baskets because they saw his resume posted on the Internet, is pure fantasy. It's the dream of every Bottom Feeder. (Which by the way is the main target of these ads.) Yes, companies do use technology to sift through the resume posting sites. But your competition is staggering. According to the book *Cyberspace Resume Kit*, the number of resumes posted on the Internet is in excess of 10.5 million and growing. You'd better know what the employer's searching software is looking for or you will be lost in the ocean of candidates.

A Shark wants only the people who can do him or her some good to see their resume. By posting on the Internet, you lose all control over who sees your resume. The shotgun approach is about as useful as putting your resume on the windshields of every car at the local mall. I remember sitting with a client in the Internet lab and he was telling me about how successful he had been because he posted his resume to the Internet. He told me he had already had nineteen hits on his resume. I asked him what kinds of companies had responded to his resume. He said, "Oh, no companies, just nineteen recruiters had taken an interest in him." That is likely to be your only response. Some recruiters will harvest the resumes and put them into their collection and then use the inflated number to try to impress businesses with the depth of their resources for finding good candidates. The success rate for people posting their resumes, unless they have such stellar credentials that are in incredibly short supply, is dismally low. For your best results, control who looks at your resume. After all, how can you do any kind of follow-up if you don't know who has seen it?

If you do still want to post your resume on the Internet, then use your head and take precautions. Limit the personal information. Give them only your name and a means to contact you. Remember you don't know who will be reviewing your resume. There are no guarantees that it will be only employers. To protect yourself, you can use an anonymous email address like Hotmail, Yahoo or several others. If it gets too clogged up with junk mail, drop it and start a new one. Another way to protect yourself is to use a pseudonym until you have an actual contact with the employer. Make sure the site that you're using to post your resume has a privacy policy that states clearly how and when your information is collected. Should you post your resume? Yes, it would be foolish to not use every available tool.

"What about sending my resume electronically?" It is quite common for employers to ask you to email your resume. Some will do it as a screening technique. If you can't do it, then you don't have the necessary computer or Internet skills required for the position. There are some basic rules you should adhere to or the results may be disastrous. Unless the employer has given you specific permission to send your resume as an attachment, do not do it. There are a few problems associated with sending your resume as an attachment. First off, how do you know they have the same program on the receiving end to open your attachment? Next, why should they trust that your attachment isn't infected with a virus?

Some people will recommend that you copy your resume from your word processing program and paste it directly into your email message box. The problem with this is that the formatting often goes out the window. What is recommended is that you create an emailable version of your resume. There are some basic steps to do this.

a) Write the resume using ASCII text. This is the style of text you see when you receive an email message.
b) Keep your margins to between 60 and 65 characters. This will prevent that scrambled look you get when the information appears in a haphazard fashion. By keeping within that range, what you see on your screen is what they will see on theirs.
c) Keep your resume simple and factual. Stick to your relevant skills, experience and qualifications. You know yourself how little you like to read page after page of email correspondence. Well, the employer likes it even less.
d) Before you email it to the employer, send it to yourself first. This will give you a chance to see what it will actually look like for the employer.

e) Keep in mind that the email address you were given probably belongs to an assistant who merely prints out the resume. Make sure your cover letter and resume are together in the one message.

f) Most important of all, make sure you're not sending along any viruses. Being known as the candidate that infected the entire network would make for a lousy first impression.

Bottom line - use the Internet if it is appropriate for your search but use it wisely.

Larry Arrance

Chapter 17. They're Free and They Work!

One of the greatest tools for getting the information that is vital to your search is going right to the source. This is what is called an informational interview. Which is an interview that you have set up with someone who can supervise or hire you or is currently holding a position to which you aspire. The reason this is so beneficial to you is that you're more likely to get the true unvarnished facts. Generally, these people have nothing to gain by giving you false information. Besides picking up valuable information, you're also expanding your list of contacts. You will find that they are quite easy to do and are often pleasurable because the environment is informal.

Unlike a regular interview, where you feel like you're in some kind of a pressure cooker because you have to impress them or they will reject you, an informational interview is a meeting with someone new. Another difference between a regular job interview and an informational interview is that you were the one that set it up. Arranging informational interviews is pure Shark behavior. They don't wait for an employer to call. Sharks call them.

Information gained by talking to insiders is quite likely to be more in-depth or completely different then what you scavenged from sources on the outside. If you're only getting your information about a company or industry from a book or article, you run the grave risk that the information is hopelessly outdated. Going to someone in the industry can give you information that is cutting edge. As a networking tool, this is one of the best because you're adding people who are a part of or are leaders in that industry. Their help could be immeasurable. But their help will only be a benefit if you're willing to follow their recommendations. If you're not going to listen, then why ask for the input? Their input as to what education or courses will be important can steer you in the right direction and help you avoid signing up for unnecessary and expensive training.

"Why would a business person give me their time for an informational interview?" There are a number of reasons people will agree to see you. For some, it could be they like to help people. Something you should keep in mind is that unemployment is something that has touched most people's lives at some point. There is a good chance that the employer or manager has gone through it himself or herself and can empathize with your situation. Others may do it from a sense of pride. Many people are proud of what they do or are proud of their company. Having you come in for an informational interview gives them an opportunity to talk about what they do. Most of them don't get the chance to talk about it to anyone else. Their friends and family have long because blocked out anything they say about their work.

Don't be surprised if your short informational interview runs overtime because sometimes it's like opening a valve to pipeline. I remember speaking with one employer, at what was scheduled as a five-minute interview, for nearly an hour. I had to finally make my escape because, based on the way he loved talking about his company, I'm sure I would still be there today. Finally, the major reason an employer agrees to doing informational interviews is that they are not job interviews. They are under no pressure to offer you a job at the end of it.

"Who should I approach?" Informational interviews are not new. Keep this in mind when you're selecting a target company. Because lots of employment counselors and job search gurus have been recommending people do them, there can be some backlash. Unfortunately, when Bottom Feeders do work up the courage to try informational interviews, they all go after the same targets. Avoid the big guns, (the big employers in your city) because, chances are, they have been informational interviewed to death. Many of them feel used and resent the steady flow of interviewees.

Consider the small and medium sized companies for your interviews. They will be able to give you information similar to the major players and are more likely to have the time available. Your potential for finding employment is also greater because they don't get the constant flood of applicants that the major companies attract. You will also strike a chord with their pride because you chose them over their towering competitors.

"How do you find out the names of these people?" The easiest way is to telephone and ask for the name.

Most companies have no reason to hide this information. Ask the receptionist for the name and correct spelling of the manager or supervisor for the position you're seeking. Then ask to be connected. When they answer go into your telephone spiel.

If you would rather go in armed with the name before you call, then you had better tap into your network of friends and find out who knows this person or at least their name and title. Ask enough people and someone will have the answer. It is a simple game of numbers. The downside to that approach is that it takes longer than just phoning the business itself. The other option it to research the business via the Internet and see if it lists its personnel. If you prefer the up-close and personal approach, you can go directly to the company and see if they keep the managers business cards on the front counter. This is the least efficient method because of the obvious time and transportation issues and there is no guarantee that the cards will be there.

"What is the best way to ask for an informational interview?" There are three methods. Cold calling in person, telephoning or in a letter. Each has its benefits and downfalls. Cold calling in person could result in an interview immediately but the chances of them being there and available are slim at best. Using your telephone spiel is faster and more efficient because you can call over twenty employers per hour. By sheer numbers alone, this is more likely to lead to success. Lastly, you can use the letter technique. For obvious reasons, this will be the most time consuming but it has its advantages. If getting through to the manager or employer is proving too difficult over the phone, then the letter may do the trick. Another reason for the letter approach is that your written skills may be stronger than your telephone technique and, therefore, more effective. This can also prove beneficial if you have a language barrier.

"How much time do I ask for?" Time is money and the employer's time should be honored. A reasonable time frame to ask for is ten to fifteen minutes. Any longer can seem like a huge imposition. It is your responsibility to keep tabs on the time. Inform them when the time you have asked for has expired and thank them for their assistance. Don't be surprised if the interview is going well and you're making a good impression on the employer that they will continue with the interview.

"How do you prepare for the interview?" Have a list of questions to ask that will give you the most useful information and that make you look intelligent at the same time. Remember that you're here to make a good impression. Focus on things about the future of the industry or their business in particular. Ask them about problems or challenges they are facing and what steps they are considering. Ask for any recommendations they may have for you concerning training or education.

Note: Handle this next suggestion with caution. Many job search professionals will recommend not bringing your resume to the interview. I think you should. I suggest presenting it if the situation feels right to you.

Other professionals warn you that producing a resume looks like you tricked them into a job interview and their reaction will be negative. You can produce the resume if it is done right and in the right context. If the person you're talking to has a solid knowledge of the industry and seems approachable, I suggest asking for their input on the content of your resume. Ask them what they think would need to be changed and what areas would be effective for their industry. You may have gone to a resume class or to a resume guru but it isn't likely that the person who helped you can know every industry and what they look for. Explain to them that you're looking for feedback and nothing else. The others suggest that you can always run home and get your resume if they ask for it but I would rather appear to be well organized with my portfolio full of every document I need for an effective job search. If you get a sense that it wouldn't be well received, then don't produce it.

"What information should I tell them?" Avoid telling them how well you would do in this position because it will come across as if you're applying for a job. Honesty is the best policy and hopefully you went into this thing with that in mind. If you honestly want information about getting into this industry because of a career change, then tell them that. If you're really looking to find out about this company and the direction it is going, then be honest about that too. Tell them you're thinking in terms of future employment. You will not be doing yourself any favors by making an employer feel duped. One of the reasons the managers or executives at the larger firms are turned off by informational interviews is that too many people claiming to be doing informational interview end up making their sales pitch for a job.

Be straight with the employer because your first priority is to build a relationship with this person. This cannot be accomplished by starting out with falsehoods and deception. During the interview, it is permissible to mention any connections or similarities there are to what is done in this industry to your old industry.

"When is the best time to meet with them?" Anytime that they are willing, obviously, but there are times that are traditionally too busy. Monday mornings are typically catch up time for most employers or managers. It is not unusual nowadays for executives to have a few hours of email correspondence to catch up on and reply to. Let them get their weekend squared away and prepared for the up coming week. Also, Friday afternoons can be a wash because they are often tying up loose ends and preparing for their weekend. On the other hand, if they offer to meet at those times don't turn them down. There is always an exception to every rule. All that counts is that you get in to see the employer.

Keep your focus on finding a time that is convenient for both of you and more importantly, them. When you're setting it up, ask for them to check their daytimer and preferably find a time in the morning. You want to meet with them before too much of their day is weighing on their minds. Employers are more impressed with someone who gets a good start on the day.

"Where should the interview take place?" Ideally, you want to meet with them in their office or in their working environment. This will give you some insight as to what goes on in the business and you want them to see you in their workplace. Also, because it is their turf, they will feel more comfortable and will associate the good feelings with you. You also want a place where there will be no interruptions. If you cannot meet at their work, then offer to buy them a coffee at a small restaurant or coffee bar. The price of a coffee, even a specialty coffee, is a small price to pay for what can be real boost to your career or job search. Even if they offer to pay, you make sure you pick up the tab. Remember they are doing you the favor. A benefit that can come from meeting them for a coffee is that there may not be any calls coming in that will have to be answered, leaving you twiddling your thumbs.

"Are there any employers I should avoid?" Common sense should be your guide here because some industries have definite criteria before you can work for them. Any medical related industry requires certain certificates or diplomas to even be considered. You will not get hired because you made a good impression and looked trainable. You will most likely be told to come back when you have the training and education. Do your research and find out what their requirements are. You might get away with doing an informational interview because you're considering going into this industry but it is just as likely that they would point you to the school that provides the courses. After all, they will have counselors who have all the information available for you. Many medical professionals complain that they get a steady stream of people who annoy them and waste their time especially when there is nothing they can do for this people anyway without the proper credentials.

"What can I expect from an informational interview?" The results can range anywhere from making a new contact for your network to an actual job offer. One of my clients wanted to make the career change from working in construction to entering the hotel and motel industry. Halfway through his third informational interview, the manager shifted into a job interview and offered him an entry-level position with the hotel. Informational interviews work. Do not underestimate their potential.

"How do I follow up?" Many informational interviews can be reduced to pretty much a waste of time if you don't do something to let them know that you appreciated their help. People are much more inclined to help you if they think you appreciated it. Have you ever helped someone only to never hear a peep out of him or her? Were you impressed? Did you feel like helping them again in the future? Send the person a card or a letter stating how much you appreciated their help. Mention any follow-up steps you're taking based upon their advice and a promise to keep them updated on your progress. These people can become powerful allies in your career change or job search. You only get the one shot at a first impression. Don't blow this one.

When you write a thank-you note be sincere and genuine. Also, it's important that the card or letter gets there very quickly. I would not wait longer than two days. You want to reinforce their memory of you as quickly as possible. I hate to burst your bubble but people can be easy to forget. So follow up on their advice, keep in contact and give sincere appreciation.

Chapter 18. "We Have Ways of Making You Talk."

Let the feasts begin. Now that your efforts are starting to bear fruits and you're getting invitations to interview for a position, what should you expect? The interview process takes on many forms because each has a different goal. Many jobs have what is a called a screening interview that is designed to see if you warrant a closer look or elimination from the list of prospects. Some companies will prefer to do this over the telephone because it is easier to toast someone when you haven't met them.

Qualifications in regards to basic skills, experience and education can be ascertained over the phone. Most of the questions will be general in nature without going into great depth. I know of one major food retailer that will conduct your first interview over the telephone. The interviewer is not a person. It will be a recording that asks you questions and you answer by choosing certain buttons on the telephone. The intent behind this type of interview is to eliminate people who can't match up their manual dexterity with rapid incoming information. This type of interview makes sense when you see how fast a checkout person must be with their fingers while inputting prices.

"What is a hiring interview? I thought they were all hiring interviews." All interviews are done with intent to see if you're worth hiring. A hiring interview quite often is done on a one-to-one basis. Your focus should be on being friendly, appearing confident and making a connection with your interviewers. They will be trying to get a good sense about you. Remember that your resume already indicated that you had the basic requirements to solve their problem, now they need to see if they get the same good feeling after talking with you. Throughout the interview, find ways to show what kind of positive results you were responsible for at your last position.

The interviewer may or may not be experienced. If they are experienced, then follow their lead but don't lose sight of the fact that you're there to sell yourself. Be sure to find a way to mention your best points and how they relate to the position. If the interviewer is not trained in interviewing, and this is often the case, then by all means take control of the interview and build a case for your product. You may even find that some interviewers are more nervous at an interview than you are. This makes total sense because they have more to lose than you do. To you this is just another job and if you don't get it, oh well. There will be other offers. For them, this is their livelihood, their business and in some cases, their entire life. Big corporations like Ford or GM can get away with hiring the odd dud but a small company with ten or less employees can suffer irreparable damage by hiring the wrong employee. So, you see, they need to be very careful in their hiring decision.

"Why a second interview? Shouldn't they just ask me all their questions the first time around?" Not everyone they interviewed the first time will be invited to the second interview. Because the number they are dealing with will be smaller, they'll have the luxury of going into greater depth with their questions. When you're in a second interview, focus on the yield that your employer enjoyed because of your efforts. Think about some of the solutions to problems that you came up with and how it benefited the company. History tends to repeat itself, so if you were successful in the past then it is easy to surmise that you will be successful in the future.

"I have heard of companies that will put you through as many as seven interviews. Is that true?" Yes, but it would only be for an upper echelon position that carries a great deal of responsibility where they can't afford to make a mistake in the hiring process. They want to place you into several different situations with different interviewers to get a much better picture of you. This will give them the opportunity to get together later and discuss what each of them saw. They will be looking for your commitment level and whether it will be enough for this position. Each interview can be treated as a weeding interview because once you make a bad impression it is extremely hard to overcome it. Interviews have been known to take place in restaurants with a slight twist involved. An interview may consist of the interviewer taking you and your entire family out to lunch. What will he learn from the experience? He will see how well you interact with your family and what kind of baggage you're bringing from home. We all have baggage. How bad is yours and is it likely to affect your work or the working environment? Some of the Bottom Feeders I have met might want to consider renting a better-behaved family for this occasion.

Another scenario could involve you being sent to dine at a very fancy restaurant along with the interviewer's wife. Guess what you will be graded on? Your table etiquette and how you conduct yourself professionally in social surroundings are what's under scrutiny. Demonstrate your self-control when it comes to alcohol consumption and be ready to make small talk. Now, this interview makes perfect sense if your position will involve wining and dining important clients. If you're a buffoon at the dinner table, you may cost the business a very important client. I have heard that 35% of executives that have lost a job opportunity because of their ill behavior at the table.

"I have heard that sometimes they will bring all the applicants into one room at the same time. What's that all about?" It is a device that can save time and money and can be much more revealing than your typical question and answer between two people. There is more than one style of group interview. Some retailers are notorious for inviting all the applicants at once and then throwing questions out into the room. The questions are not directed at any one person. The people who respond to this type of questioning are extroverts. It is a simple system for separating outgoing individuals who are more likely to interact quickly with customers from quiet ones who will be reluctant to approach someone else.

A good friend of mine was invited to such a group interview at a chiropractor's office. She had an advantage over the other people who came to the interview. My friend had been to this type of interview before and knew what strategy she would have to use to win the position. Because she knew that the entire process was part of the interview she put on her game face and went to work. She knew that when they were outside waiting to be invited in, they were being observed. Understanding this and that to be successful in the position she was applying for, she would have to appear friendly and outgoing. So, she made a point of striking up conversations with the other applicants and giving out lots of smiles. Once inside the doors, she made sure she continued with the extra effort to connect with those sitting around her. When the interviewer started pelting the group with questions, she made sure she was the most prominent one answering. The result was that she was rewarded with the position.

A major airline has been known to use the same type of interviewing practice with the exception being that the people evaluating your performance are hidden away behind a two-way mirror. Unfortunately, you cannot tell what they are grading you on and you can't tell if you're doing well or not.

Another type of group interview that I took part in was extremely effective. It consisted of having all sixteen applicants brought into one room. I prefer to call them contestants because only one will walk away with the position. They were then placed around tables in groups of four. Each group was to play a game based upon some type of disaster. The interviewers didn't do anything except observe the players. It was amazing to see how quickly you could accurately size up an individual. I watched a table that had two men and two women. The two men were butting heads as to what should be done first. Each man wanted to be in charge and wasn't willing to back down. At another table, nothing was happening. There were four very passive people and no one wanted to take charge. Finally, the least passive of them got the ball rolling. The process was very revealing. You could tell who was a leader, who was a tyrant, who followed well, who took initiative, and who gave up easily. Each personality rose quickly to the surface. If you ever find yourself in this situation, remember why you're there and act accordingly to impress the observers.

"I was at an interview once and the interviewer seemed really nasty. I was so intimidated that I virtually froze. What should I have done?" Well, you may have run into a naturally nasty person. They are out there but usually they are, or were, related to you through marriage. In all likelihood, you were the victim of what is called the stress interview. I know they all seem like stress interviews but this one is designed to assess where your ability to handle stressful situations. It is very unlikely that the person actually doesn't like you. It is just part of the strategy. They will seem to be very aggressive and confrontational towards you. It is important that you keep your sense of humor and not get defensive. This style of interview is unlikely, unless the position you're seeking involves high levels of stress. They need to make sure you don't go postal when the pressure mounts. They need to how you're likely to react.

Make sure you remain as personable and professional as is possible. Remember you're here to sell yourself not get into an argument with the interviewer. You might want to ask yourself after the interview if you would want to be part of an organization that would treat people this way. Remember, you're there to see if they are right for you, too.

"What if the interview takes place at a restaurant?" Focus on why you're there. This is not a social get together it is an interview. The meal interview can be used to get you to lower your guard because you're in a situation outside the normal interview process. Be very aware of your dining etiquette. Do not order anything that has the potential to be messy. It's hard to make a good impression with something disgusting stuck between your teeth or dribbling down your clothes. They will be picking up the tab for the meal and will be watching which item you choose. Don't order the most expensive item on the menu. They may think that you will be that free with their company assets as well. When it comes to ordering drinks, walk a cautious line. Don't order alcohol unless the interviewer does. When your drink comes, nurse it slowly throughout the meal. Getting tipsy won't help your cause. If you're a non-drinker, choose a non-alcoholic beverage but don't make a big deal about being an abstainer because you don't know their feelings on the subject.

"Is it true that some interviews might be taped?" Having a video camera in the room may be done for a couple of reasons. First, they may actually be taping the interview so that they can study it later. This is done quite often if the position involves dealing with children. The interviewer or interviewers can study the videotape later to look for any non-verbal communication or inconsistencies in your answers. This is done to screen out potential threats to children. Of course, they will seek your permission before the camera is turned on. If you refuse, then you have probably eliminated yourself.

Now, many of us hate being in front of the camera and can become more nervous than usual. Tell them this fact and ask them to take it into consideration. Ignore the camera if you can but if you cannot then pretend it is just another person in the room. Focus on the interview and the process of describing the benefits you're bringing to the job.

Another reason for a camera being at an interview is that there may be a videoconference taking place with someone in authority who could not physically be there. Again, treat the camera as if it were a real person and make eye contact with it when you answer a question. The interview process does not change. You're still there to sell yourself.

"At one interview they had me do a series of tests." This is what we call ability testing. Basically, they want to see if you can walk your talk. You will be given tasks that will determine if you have the necessary skills to be successful in the position. The tests or tasks can be very apparent to the position or make no sense at all to you. When someone comes to an interview with our office in the capacity of administration support, they'll be given a computer and a resume and told to reproduce it. It will be part of their duties to be able to produce resumes for our clients. Ability tests show, you can do more than just talk a good game. One of my clients used to manage a construction company. She said that when someone would apply for a carpenter's or laborer's position, she would point to a pile of lumber and tell them that they have twenty minutes to build two saw horses. She said that building the sawhorses was a basic skill and if they couldn't do that then they obviously weren't qualified to do anything else either.

An owner of a gymnasium in Yellow Knife, Northwest Territories, said that when she interviewed people for a personal fitness trainer position she assigned them a client. The applicant would provide two hours of personal training and develop a fitness routine for that client. The applicant would be doing it for free. She felt that a good employee would be willing to prove themselves and be willing to invest a little of their time in the process. If she liked the way the applicant worked with the client and was willing to bring her into her business, she would give her one more assignment. She would ask the applicant to go home and think about it for forty-eight hours. If they still wanted the job, then the position was theirs. The owner said that with such a small population, she couldn't afford to hire the wrong person and risk a poor employee driving away clientele. That's why she needed to know that the fit worked both ways.

Other ability tests could involve answering questionnaires, quizzes or tests. Depending on the position you're going after it, could involve math questions or problem solving such as they would require of applicants for an Air Traffic Controller position. Some companies will incorporate a battery of tests to determine multiple things about your strengths and weaknesses. What they will have done is give the same tests to their best employees and then see how close you come to their scores. The idea behind this is that if your score is similar then you must be pretty close to the same kind of worker. I think their theory has a few flaws to it. Another questionable device is the honesty test. The creators of this interesting concept took a questionnaire and had professionals answer the questions and then had the same questionnaire completed by inmates of correctional centers. The theory behind it is if your score is closer to the professionals then you must be more honest than someone who scored closer to the prisoners. I was once told by a law enforcement official that the only difference between the people in prison and those on the outside was that the first group got caught.

Unfortunately, you can lose a job opportunity based on some questions that seem to have very little to do with honesty. One such question is "Would you like to try sky diving?" A positive answer means you're honest and a negative answer indicates you shouldn't be trusted. I guess all those people who are afraid of heights are liars and thieves. Studies of the test results have shown that sometimes as many as one hundred percent of the respondents thought it was okay to take stuff home from the company if they believed the business owed them more than they were getting. Would it alter the results if a liar lied when he answered the questions? Isn't that what liars do?

Being prepared for an ability test is your best bet for improved performance. Ask the interviewer when they call to set up an interview, what type of interview process they'll be using. Many will let you know what to expect. Tell them you believe in being prepared. They may give you points for thinking ahead and being proactive.

"I went to an interview once and there was more than one person asking me questions. Is that typical?" This is called a panel interview and you're likely to see more of them. Many businesses are encouraging their management staff to incorporate the panel interview. It can be highly beneficial to the company because they get away from having only one person's input for each position. I remember going to a Christmas function with my wife. It was her first year with the company. She pointed out one of the tables where about eight women were sitting. She indicated that they were all from the same department. I started to laugh because they all looked like they were poured from the same mould. They were all about the same height and weight. All were attractive. I said, "let me guess, it is the same guy that hires for that department, right?" It turned out that I was correct. When that manager left the company the department became more diverse.

By doing to a panel interview, they can get away from singular thinking. The other benefit of a panel interview is that it protects the backside of the company. Nowadays, if I'm interviewing someone and I end up not choosing him or her for whatever reason, I stand a good chance of finding myself in court. If someone decides that I was discriminating against them, they might try suing the company for damages. A panel interview eliminates this problem because it is unlikely that everyone had a problem with that applicant.

Do not change your game plan too much for the one-on-one or the panel interview. Remember, you're still there to highlight reasons why you're right for this position. The only real difference is that you won't expend a great deal of energy trying to make a connection with the interviewer. Panels can be two and up to as many as six or more people. It is unlikely that you can establish rapport that quickly with that many different personalities. Ideally, you want to turn and face the person who asked you the question. If they asked it, then the chances are very good that it was a concern of theirs. If you do feel that one of them is obviously the top dog, you can direct your answers to this person. Or if you find that one of them is very warm and cordial towards you, direct your responses to them. This may help you relax.

If it seems that one of them has a real mad-on for you, it is probably a role that they were assigned. This is another attempt at turning up the pressure on you. Don't take it personally. Keep your wits about you and answer the questions just as if they were asked in a friendly manner. If you find the person is asking you new questions before you have finished your previous question, be firm and let them know that you will answer each question in its entirety before you handle the next one. Keep your sense of humor about it, after all it is just an interview, in reality your entire life or career doesn't rest solely on this job interview. There will be others.

Other panel interviews may seem like sitting in front of an oil painting pretending to be a panel. You will often experience this type of panel when you're applying for a government position. They are sometimes coached to give you zero feedback so that you don't know if you're doing well or not. The object is to keep you off balance. Don't panic. Just follow your game plan for letting them know why you're right for the job.

"Somebody told me they went on a relocation interview. What's that about?" These are done when the position is a great distance from where you live. You will have likely gone through an initial screening interview either over the phone or by a representative in the region. They will fly you into their city for the interview. Many people get really nervous because they are off their own turf. The company is going to give you an in-depth interview to test your commitment and worth before going to the expense of relocating you to this area. They will be focused on any obstacles that might prevent you from making the move successfully. They could be concerned about your family commitments and if they are willing to make the move also. It is very costly for them if you don't stay long enough for them to recoup their investment. You had better be able to convince them of your flexibility and adaptability. Make sure you're excited about the position and see it as an opportunity not an inconvenience.

"How do I prepare for a telephone interview?" Telephone interviews can be tricky because most of us present ourselves better in person where our non-verbal communication skills enhance the message. The key here is to be as professional as possible. Remember that the phone is a very precise instrument. The caller can hear if you're breathing hard, smoking, eating or chewing gum. Eliminate any distractions such as children, pets or television sets. If you have been caught at an awkward time, then ask if you can call back in a few minutes so that you take care of the situation and give your best to the interviewer. Keep all your materials such as your resume and credentials handy so that you can refer to them. Remember to smile. Write down the person's name so that you can use it during the interview. Focus on describing why you're the ideal person for this position. Your goal is to get to the in-person interview.

Chapter 19. Be as SEXY as You Can and Make Your Answers PAY.

Judgment Day has arrived! The day you have longed for, sought after, did everything in your power to create, has arrived at last and now you're sweating puddles. Being nervous is normal being unprepared is stupid. If you have been following the advice that I have given you so far, this shouldn't be an ordeal. It should be looked upon as an adventure. First step is to not increase the pressure on yourself by thinking you have to walk away with a job offer. Instead, focus on telling the interviewer why you have a good product and finding out more about their company. Those are two things you have some control over.

If we were in my classroom right now you would be taking part in a brainstorming session to compile a list of commonly asked questions. Regardless of whether my group comes up with twenty or two hundred, it doesn't matter. What you will find is that it can be reduced down to two simple lists of three. First we look at the three basic types of questions you will face: open, closed and leading. The open question can be a Godsend or a death sentence. To a Shark the open-ended question lets them take control and package their answer to best suit their needs. To a Bottom Feeder, this question makes it glaringly clear that they are unprepared. Because the open question does not have any parameters the Bottom Feeder does one of two things. They will answer the question in the fewest words possible and accomplish nothing or they will ramble on and on until the interviewer has forgotten what they asked.

The second type of question is the closed. These are your typical yes or no questions. You won't impress anyone with either of those answers because they don't create much of a picture. Let's imagine that I ask you "Have you ever had your driver's license revoked?" You reply "No." Have you sold me anything? A Shark would have answered with "No, because I treat my license like it is one of my tools. I treat it with respect and can assure you that I have a clean driving record." Now, the Shark has sold you his mature and responsible attitude towards his driving and his work.

The third type is the Leading question. You're not likely to run into this type of question unless you're up against a very seasoned interviewer. The interviewer will try to lead you into disclosing something that you would prefer to not admit. For example, "You must have found that during the Christmas season rush that sometimes work got pretty hectic?" By now in the interview, you have been so focused on being agreeable and connecting with the interviewer that you're starting to resemble one of the toy dogs in the back of a car window who's head continually bounces up and down. And you answer. "Yeah, sometimes it was pretty crazy. Those crowds can really be something else." The interviewer just got you to admit that you get stressed when the pressure is on. A Shark would answer "Actually we kept the department very organized and were prepared for the extra crowds. I found it quite exciting to handle that much business." Remember, you have to come out on the positive end of things with every question.

The second group of three is basically the types of information they are after. Can you do the job? Are you willing to do the job? Will you fit in?

Every question the interviewer asks communicates a concern about you're your ability to do the job. Regardless of what kind of package the interview wraps the concern in; it will still be the same concern. Quite often when the class is deep into their brainstorming session someone will challenge one of the questions that was added to the list. They will say that companies can't ask certain questions because they're illegal. I tell them not to waste energy worrying about illegal questions. Try to uncover the concern for the interviewer that prompted the question. You will not be offered a position by challenging the interviewer. If the interviewer asks about your children, what is their concern? They are afraid that your children will prove to be a huge distraction and you will not be able to make it to work. If you can't make it to work, you can't do the job. It's the same if they ask about your transportation. What's their concern? If you can't make it to work, you can't do the job. It's that simple. Answer the concern. Explain how you have your daycare arranged and how it has never been a problem in the past. As for your transportation, tell them the method or methods that you will use to make it to work on time and every time.

If the interviewer continues to ask you questions that you consider inappropriate, then you need to reconsider if you actually want to work for that company or not. One of my clients, who by the way is a very attractive young woman, applied for position with a restaurant located up at a ski resort. The manager asked her how often her boyfriend would come by to visit her. Red flags started popping up and rightly so. This guy was heading into territory that was way out of bounds. Because she had never mentioned having a boyfriend, it seemed obvious that his mind wasn't entirely on how well she could handle the job. In this case, the interviewer flunked the interview.

The are you willing questions, divulge your work ethic and how flexible you're about working to their schedule. You will get questions about shift work, relocation or furthering training or education. Everybody has some sort of personal restrictions as to when and where they can work. Just be aware that the more restrictions you have the less opportunities may be available for you.

Have you ever worked someplace where someone did not fit in? What was the result? Aggravation, disruption, dissention and general loss in productivity are the byproducts of a poor fitting employee. That is why an interviewer has to determine how well you will fit in. The questions can be as straightforward as "How do you get along with people?" to questions about salary or even to the seemingly bizarre "If you were an animal, what would you be?" What the interviewer wants to know is that you got along with your last coworkers and likely to get along with new ones. Take the salary question, for instance. If your idea of a fair wage is light years away from all the rest of the staff, then there might be concern if you're going to fit in with the way the others think. The animal question is more of a psychological question. Some interviewers think that the person will pick an animal that closely resembles their own personality traits or is something they aspire to.

Using one of my female students as an example, I told the class that she had always seen herself as an eagle. She was amazed because that is exactly as she had seen herself. Trust me, it was just dumb luck on my part. I then asked the class to tell me what attributes they connected with an eagle. They said things like aggressive, powerful, loner and predatory. The young lady was aghast at the description. That was not how she described an eagle. To her they were regal, majestic, powerful and intelligent. I then asked the group how they would they feel about someone who chose an eagle, if they were hiring for a daycare? Would they get a warm and fuzzy feeling? When a Shark answers this question they choose an animal that has the characteristics that are likely to lead to success in the position. They don't let the interviewer draw their own conclusions, tell them why you chose that animal and what positive characteristics the creature displays.

There are far too many questions that might come your way for me to list them in this book but it doesn't matter. Just take any question you can think of and dissect it until you know what a possible concern is and then eliminate that concern.

Here are some of the most basic questions:

"Tell me about yourself." This is a good example of an open question. You should expect this question because it is a very natural one. After all, you're the expert on the subject. Be prepared. Keep to your professional life. The personal stuff will be most likely to kill you. Don't bother telling where you were born or about your family. Focus on your work life and how it makes you right for this position. I recommend you use this simple format. I HAVE, I CAN, I'M. The "I Have" section tells them about qualifications such as education, training, and experience you have that make you right for the job. The "I Can" section gives examples of your skills in regards to things you can do like selling, building, teaching, etc. The "I Am" section describes all your personal attributes like team player, dedication and all those other warm and fuzzy things that make you so special. By packaging your material in this manner, you control how the information comes out and eliminate tougher questions later.

Let's imagine that you're sitting in front of your television and a commercial for Volvo comes on. Now there are probably a hundred good reasons for someone to buy a Volvo. Will they tell you all one hundred in the commercial? No, because it would be too much and you couldn't absorb it all. Successful commercials are based on clearly communicating a select few benefits repeatedly. I always recommend that my clients know five solid reasons why they are right for the position before they go to the interview. Throughout the interview, refer back to those five reasons. At the end of the interview, the employer will know five solid reasons why you would be right for their company. Your competition won't be that organized. Describing your five reasons should take less than one minute per reason. Doing this exercise is very beneficial to you because it solidifies in your mind why you're right for the job. This preparation will greatly diffuse your nervousness.

"What is your greatest strength?" Asking for your greatest strength, indicates that they only want the one answer. You can, however, enhance your answer by adding a few extra strengths. "Besides my strong communication skills and my ability to close a sale, I would have to say my greatest strength is my ability to cold call and generate leads." You just slipped three strengths for the price of one.

"What is your greatest weakness?" This question is like the kiss of death for a Bottom Feeder because they often have too many to choose from and are tempted to share all of them. The employer wants to know what your weakness is because it might prove to be disastrous to the company. I had a client who told me his greatest weakness was alcohol. Wow. With great answers like that it's hard to believe he was unemployed! Another reason the employer asks this question, is to see if you can identify your weakness and whether you are taking any steps to correct the situation. A Shark will take his or her weakness and turn it into a selling point. The first thing a Shark will do is make sure they never repeat the word "weakness." When someone tells you about their weakness, do they come across in a positive light? It is like the person who says they have a weakness for chocolate. Do they ever get past that weakness? No, it's theirs for life.

Instead, use an answer that replaces the word *weakness* with *challenge* or *area of development*. The latter two words give you a sense that the person can overcome this situation and be better for it. Example: "My greatest challenge has always been becoming too enthusiastic about a project and taking on too much of the responsibility. I have learned to be more realistic about my contribution and let the rest of the team do their share too. This allows me to turn in a much better product." There won't be many employers who would be turned off by you being a Keener.

"What are you looking for in the way of salary?" Tread very carefully here. Before you go to an interview you should have done your research on what the industry pays. There are numerous sites on the Internet that will give you pay scales for your area. The only time you should mention a dollar figure is when you already know what they pay for that position. The hazard of giving a dollar figure without knowing what they pay can led to one of two mistakes. Your price is too high and you just priced your product out of the market or your price is too low and you have undervalued your product. It isn't likely that they will pick you up at the lower price because they will think that you're not up to their standards.

While doing a mock interview with one of my students, I asked him the salary question. He responded with "$10.00 per hour." I was a little taken aback because we had just gone over the fact that you don't name an exact sum. He went on to explain that he had just started attending a church and there was a young woman there that he would like to date. He figured he would need $10.00 per hour to do it properly. As the mock employer, I was happy he hadn't picked one of the $15.00 per hour women because we couldn't afford that!

Shark's answer: "My research showed that the industry standard for this region is between 40 and 60 thousand dollars. With the training and experience I have, I'm sure we will find a number that we will both be happy with. We can discuss that upon hiring." Some questions are like bombs - they can blow up in your face. If someone hands me a bomb, I will hand it right back to him or her. "When I was doing my research I wasn't able to establish what your going rate is for this position. What do you pay someone in this position?" If they press you for an actual sum and you're still not sure about an appropriate salary, then give them back the bomb. "Are you offering me this position at this time?" Now there's a good chance that she wasn't ready to make that move yet and will now have to back pedal. "No, I was just trying to establish what your salary expectations were." And you reply: "Well I don't know enough about the responsibilities and expectations for this position to give you a fair price. We can discuss the salary upon hiring."

I could go on with hundreds more questions but we don't need to if you master the next two techniques.

Technique number one is being as *sexy* as possible. Before you call me a sexist pig, I'm not talking about wearing short skirts and showing lots of cleavage. That technique doesn't work. Well, let's just say it never worked for me. Sexy is a formula. It stands for Skills, Example and Yield. When answering a question, think of the skill it demonstrates, give an example of where you used it and tell them what the yield was. Your typical Bottom Feeder will answer a question in the fewest words possible. Quite often this is done because they just want the interview finished so they can escape. A Shark knows that every question is a sales opportunity.

Bottom Feeder answer – "I have strong organizational skills." How does that answer make you feel? They are just words. They haven't given you any reason to believe them.

Shark answer – "I have strong organizational skills. When I was hired into the sales department, I went through the files and compiled a list of all the old customers of the sales people who were no longer with the company. I systematically contacted each of the past customers to establish a relationship. This generated enough sales leads that by my third month with the company I took the Sales Person of the month award." This answer demonstrated that the person was both organized and self-motivated. Bonus!

Technique number two is to say what they need to hear. Pay is another formula. P stands for problem, A stands for action you took, and Y stands for the yield. Example question – "Do you work better as part of a team or alone?"

Bottom Feeder answer – "I can do either."
Shark answer – "When I was in university I tended to do work on my own and was maintaining very good grades. My professor gave us a project that required working with a partner. In the beginning, it seemed like we would never agree on anything and were not likely to successfully complete our assignment. I understood that most disagreements stem from a breakdown in communication, so we approached it one last time. When we sat down and made a list of what we agreed on, we found out that we weren't all that far apart after all. It was a matter of both making concessions until we found a solution we were happy with. We both received top marks for our project." The answer demonstrates that the person can work effectively in either realm and can take constructive steps to solve problems.

Create a list of problems you or your department has faced and what action steps you took to solve it and what the yield was. You should be able to build a healthy arsenal of examples that demonstrate vividly your history of solving problems.

Never give an answer that doesn't have a story attached to it because it's the story that sells every time. Everything else is just words. My class and I were watching a taped interview of one of their classmates. This fellow had been answering every question with abrupt or bland answers. They were starting to slip into boredom-induced comas until he answered a question with a story. The room sat up in unison and paid attention. They later said they would have hired him based on that one answer.

Often clients will ask me about handling difficult questions. The only time a question is difficult for you is when you haven't made yourself comfortable with it. They have a saying in sales "If you have a problem with your product, you will find a way to bring it into the conversation." I know this from experience. I tried the network marketing experience. I proved that I'm no good at it. My belief about the product was that it was too pricey. The product was great but I felt that they had inflated the price to cover all the commissions. My wife on the other hand thought the price was fair. She had no problem at all making sales. Because I thought the price was too high, when potential buyers were trying to purchase the product from me I would find a way to scuttle the sale. They could have their checkbook out and I would find a way to give them the product instead. Needless to say, my wife strongly suggested I get out of the business.

You'll know if you have a problem with your product if you've ever thought; "I hope they don't ask me about _____." Whatever statement you write into the blank, is something you'll have to address. You need to be able to take that problem and spin it around. Make it into a selling point. That way, if the question comes up, you can answer it. If it doesn't come up, it won't matter because you can answer it. One client was worried about age discrimination. The obvious solution was to create a list of reasons why their age was a benefit. Things like no daycare problems, experience in many areas, less transient than young employees and the list goes on from there.

If your difficult question involves something negative, then prepare an answer that shows you take responsibility and then tell them what you learned and how it makes you a better person or employee. Everyone makes mistakes but only the smart ones learn from them. Management firms have been known to pass over candidates that have not experienced any major setbacks in their careers or lives. The reasoning is that it is those experiences that develop our character and add to our knowledge base. Someone who has seen a bankruptcy up close and personal has picked up a lot more valuable education in what not to do than someone who merely read about it in a book. Quite often what we perceive as a detriment can actually be an asset. Who often goes on to be excellent addiction counselors? That's right, ex-addicts because they know what they're talking about because they have been there. Their detriment became their biggest asset. So take your so-called detriment and reshape and repackage it until it will be seen as a benefit.

"What if they consider me to be overqualified?" The reasons why this might bother an interviewer: the job might be beneath you and you will get bored and leave for a better job or your credentials threaten their job. Your main job is to eliminate the threat of you leaving and them wasting the their investment of training you or your staying and possibly going after their job. Let them know that they'll be getting a Cadillac for the price of a dune buggy. Focus on all the different ways that your wealth of experience and knowledge can be tapped into and utilized. If the position is beneath your normal duties and you're fine with it, let them know why. Maybe you're no longer interested in the climbing of the success ladder and have got to point in your career where contributing to the growth and success of a company are reward enough. To calm the fears of an insecure supervisor, let them know that you're not seeking a management position but if the need ever arose and they needed someone to fill that role, you would be glad to help. You have to show them as many ways possible how their lives would be better with you around.

"What if I can't think of an answer to one of their questions?" We all suffer from brain glitches from time to time and especially when we are nervous. Unless the question is an easy one like "What's your name?" which you should have practiced on the way over, it's okay to admit that you've drawn a blank. Tell them you're slightly nervous and ask them to take that into consideration. Ask them if you can come back to it later. On the notepad that you have brought with you, make a quick note about the question. That marvelous mind of yours will process the information and after a few more questions, the answer will be available. Make sure you come back to it. Every question is an opportunity to sell your product. Don't miss any of them.

Larry Arrance

Chapter 20. Okay It's My Turn.

Employers and managers expect you to have questions because it shows you're serious about your career and you don't just jump at any employment opportunity. Their fear may be that you don't put much thought into your decisions. You will start working for them, they will put training dollars into you and then you come to the conclusion that this isn't what you were looking for. Now they are out the costs of interviewing, hiring, training and get to begin the process all over again. Your questions will also tell them how much effort you put into researching the company.

Bottom Feeders quite often do not have questions and when they do they focus on what they are going to get from the employer. Asking about wages, benefits and perks before they have offered you the position, is just stupid. Hopefully, throughout the interview, you have kept your focus on what you will do for them. This is not the time to shift the conversation to what's in it for you. Their head is still occupied with whether or not you would be a good acquisition. Putting on your greed cap can sour the good feeling you worked so hard at creating.

Don't ask questions that you should already know the answer to from your research. Nowadays, with most companies being connected to the *information highway*, employers will expect you to have at least done your basic research.

Larry Arrance

Focus your questions around what kind of challenges you will be facing in the first year and what kind of expectations the company has for your performance. Find out what kind of a supervisor you will be working with and if there is a chance to meet with them after the interview. Ask them if there are any special projects coming up that they think you would be especially well suited to handle. Find out what the last person did that made them successful or unsuccessful. Find out ahead of time what is appreciated and what is frowned upon.

Finding out why the last person left could prove to be highly beneficial. There may be a very good reason why this position is available and it may not be a positive one. For what seemed like forever, there was an ad that ran in a local paper asking for a sales clerk in a little shoe store. The ad never seemed to be out of the paper for more than a couple of weeks. When there is a heavy turnover in a business, little red warning signs should pop up for you. Why are people being rotated through the position? They can't all be lousy employees. Do you want to be a part of the exodus?

Creating an image that you will be successful and do the job well is important both to you and the interviewer. Ask questions that will create an opportunity to show you have the potential. "What attributes and skills would the ideal candidate possess to be successful in this position?" As they list them off, make a mental list. When they are done, give

230

examples of how you have demonstrated those in the past.

If you're in an interview based upon an advertisement, you better make sure you give the impression you studied the job description. "I noticed in the job description that you listed computer skills ahead of all the other requirements. How important is teamwork and communication skills to this position?" It will be important to them on some level. Even if the position is primarily working alone, you're likely to interact and communicate with others at some point. Expand on how effective you were in your past job utilizing your communication and interpersonal skills.

You're going to be judged on your ability to grow in the position. This doesn't necessarily mean promotions. You have to expect that there will be new responsibilities that will eventually be attached to the position. Ask questions that will give you the opportunity to demonstrate how quickly you learn new skills or how much you enjoy new challenges. "In what ways could you see this position changing in the future?"

Let the interviewer understand how important you consider being properly trained for the position. If their job description mentions a training period or ongoing training, ask for details about it. Sometimes companies won't have a budget set aside for training. So don't leave them with a negative feeling about your possible disappointment in their lack of investment in their employees. Show them that you take the

231

responsibility for keeping your education updated. "With my last employer they had a limited budget for training. I gladly accepted what they did have to offer and supplemented it with training courses I purchased on my own."

It's always a good idea to know what an employer expects of you and what you should expect your typical workday or week to be. Ask questions concerning who will supervise, what you will be doing and how your performance will be evaluated. "I had a client who had been blindsided in her job. She had been hired for one position and then given the duties of another position that demanded a much higher skill level. Naturally, she floundered because of the inability to do the job adequately and they fired her. Know what they expect of you. Make sure it is reasonable and you're not setting yourself up for a failure.

Whenever you get an answer to your questions, find a way to connect your skills, abilities or experience to it. If they tell you what a typical day's duties would be, explain how you have done the same or similar duties in another position.

I mentioned earlier that you should take a note pad to the interview. One of the reasons for this is so you can write you question down. The faintest ink is still better than the best memory because it isn't going anywhere. When you're nervous, you have a greater chance of forgetting something. The pad won't let you.

If you have done your homework and have researched the position and business, you will have better questions to ask. Be like a lawyer. Don't ask questions unless you already know the answer. Example: if you ask about possibilities for advancement and the company is small and the only way up is to marry the employer, you have just created an image that says you're too ambitious. If there is nowhere to go, then you're likely to be frustrated. The employer may think that you're a risky investment and you always look for greener pastures.

One of the best questions I was ever asked by a client during a mock interview was "Of all my qualifications, which one do you think will make me a success in this position?" Brilliant! She had me helping her to sell the product to myself. I was forced to quickly summarize her qualifications in order to answer her question.

Don't underestimate people's fondness for talking about themselves and the work they do. It is acceptable to ask the interviewer how they got their start in the industry. A note of caution here – if the interviewer's last name is the same as the company's, there may be some sensitivity as to having had their position handed to them. If that isn't a consideration, then you could ask them what steps they took to advance to their present position and whether the opportunity to enjoy that kind of career advancement is still possible.

If you have noticed or heard that people enjoy working for this company, ask them what it is about working there that keeps the staff happy. On the other hand, if you haven't got a sense that people are happy in their work or the social aspects of this company, why are you applying here? When they tell you the good points, connect to it with "This sounds like a great place work. I would enjoy being a part of it."

If you have developed skills or demonstrated strengths in volunteer or professional organizations, see if there is a way to bring it into the conversation. Ask them if the company encourages involvement in the community or belonging to professional associations. Tell them what you have gained from the experience that has made you a better and more valuable employee.

Nothing is perfect - including the job opportunity. Don't be afraid of asking questions about the possible negative aspects this position may have. "Every job has aspects that aren't as appealing as others. Is there anything that I should be concerned about?" When they answer, let them know that you have done those things before and they don't really bother you.

Finding out why customers choose to do business with their company can uncover a couple pieces of valuable information. It will tell you why the interviewer is proud of the company and what the business's philosophy is concerning what's important, customer service or sales. Naturally, you will connect with their answer. If you were highly successful in the customer service arena then give examples. Or, if you have a stellar sales record, bring that back into the conversation.

We live in a world of outsourcing and contracting out. Do they have a history of this practice and could this position be in jeopardy? "I've read articles about many of the operations that were typically done in-house throughout the industry that have been outsourced. Is there much likelihood that this position could fall victim to the same fate?"

Maybe you're going after a management position. Find out what the employer's expectations are concerning the development of your staff. What kind of budget or resources will be made available to you? Ask them what you can expect in the way of acceptance and cooperation when you come in as a manager of an established workplace. Ask for any suggestions they have for making the transition smoother.

Your research may have told you about a new product, service or project the company is undertaking. Ask them questions that could connect you to it. "From articles I've read I understand that you're developing a smaller and more affordable All Terrain Vehicle. Will I be able to make a contribution towards its success?"

"I want the position. How do I let them know?" Hopefully, you have been acting eager about the position all the way through the interview. Employers don't like rejection any better than you do. They might be hesitant about offering the position to you if they don't have some idea that you want it. There are a number of ways to get the message across that you want the job. The easiest is to be blunt. Tell them "this position seems like a great match for my skills and abilities. I'm very interested in the position." No guess work there for them.

Ask them a question. "What is the next step in the interview process? Will there be another interview? I'm available if you need more information." If you're really gutsy and you have developed some rapport with the interviewer, try a humorous approach. "The position sounds just right for me. When do I start?" Or "Based upon what we have discussed so far, are you considering me for this position?"

If you're in sales and you don't ask for the position, what have you told them? Is this passive approach typical of your sales approach? A salesperson that doesn't ask for the position isn't much of a salesperson. Even if you don't consider yourself a salesperson, you're better off taking the more aggressive approach. What is the worst that can happen? They may say no - but at least you know where you stand. Chances are you, didn't get the position anyway. You can now invest all your energies into the next interview.

Chapter 21. Where Bottom Feeders Kill Themselves.

Easy question for you "How many chances to you get to make a first impression?" Most Bottom Feeders don't get this question right. Some of them think that it's like baseball with the "three strikes and you're out rule". Studies have shown that most interviewers make up their minds within a couple of minutes into the interview. They will spend the rest of the interview trying to justify their decision.

"When should I arrive for an interview?" There is a saying in the employment industry. "If you're on time for an interview, you're already late." You need to arrive at least ten minutes early for the interview. This will give you time to locate the nearest washroom and make sure your appearance is perfect. You don't want to be in an interview and start worrying about what your hair looks like because it was windy outside or if you have something stuck in your teeth. I know of a job applicant who arrived for the interview right at the appointed time. She was ushered promptly into the office. One of the interviewers told me later that it was very difficult to focus on her answers because his eyes occupied with the pile of bird crap on her shoulder. Apparently, a bird anointed her on her trip from the car to the front door. Always make sure your accessories are appropriate to the interview!

"How should I dress for the interview?" Many of the books that describe appropriate dress for interviews seem to think that everyone works in an office. Can you wear blue jeans to an interview? Sure, it would depend on the job. Your smartest bet is to do your research. Phone and ask the receptionist what the dress code is or take a trip there ahead of time and scout out what the locals are wearing. There is a rule of thumb for interviews. Dress like them but a notch above. If you go to extremes and wear a fancy dress or a three-piece suit for a position that is definitely blue collar, you run the risk of them thinking you're a fish out of water. You want to be seen as one of them.

"How friendly should I be?" Use your common sense. If I go into an office, I tell them who I'm and why I'm there and let the front office staff set the friendliness tone. If I go in there and come across as a super friendly "Chatty Cathy" doll, I run the risk of annoying them. These people are working. They have jobs to do. Monopolizing their time can be seen as an irritant. If they strike up a conversation, then I will respond in kind. Otherwise, I will ask where I can sit until the interview and I will spend the time focusing on doing well in the interview.

"What should I take to the interview?" Unfortunately, sometimes the infamous Mr. Murphy will go to the job interview with you. My advice is to not take anything to an interview that you don't need at an interview. A client was telling me that she went to an interview and was quite nervous. She rested her purse against the leg of the chair. Because she was fidgeting in her chair, she didn't notice that the chair leg had snagged the handle of the purse. When she stood up to leave, she grabbed her purse. The contents of the purse exploded into the room. There are some things in a woman's purse that not everybody needs to be aware of. Needless to say, both parties were embarrassed and uncomfortable.

"Should I shake hands or not?" In Europe, it's not uncommon for coworkers to shake hands several times throughout the day according to the coming and going. In North America, it can be a bit of a rarity. I have worked with some of the same people for close to ten years. I doubt if we have shaken hands more than five times. Don't take it for granted that everybody shakes hands. Let the interviewer initiate the handshake. If they do at the beginning of the interview, then you initiate it at the end of the interview.

"What if they offer me a coffee?" Unless you're at a restaurant, do not accept it. Remember Mr. Murphy? There's a good chance that you will be nervous. When you're nervous, your bladder may already be working overtime. Does it make sense to add caffeine to the mix? If the interview runs longer than you expected, you could run into bladder overload. Now your focus is gone. All you will want to do right then is escape to the washroom. Another reason for not accepting coffee is that professional interviewers will offer it as a set up. When you receive your coffee, it will be filled to the brim. It is no longer a cup of coffee but a biofeedback device. They'll watch the top of the coffee as they ask you questions. Your negative or positive reaction to the question will register on the surface of the coffee in the form of ripples or even whitecaps. So remember, if it doesn't improve your interview presentation, you don't need it.

"How much eye contact do I need to make?" Depending on cultural considerations, you want to pay special attention to your eye contact. You don't have to lock eyes with them until one of them flinches but you should be able to make eye contact when you answer the question. If you can't look them in the eye when you answer, they may think you're lying or have something to hide. It's okay to look away from the interviewer from time to time but make sure you do make contact during the delivery of the answer.

"I have been warned about using the wrong body language. What should I worry about?" First off, worrying about it is a waste of energy. I read a newspaper column that recommended people sit a certain way in a chair during the interview. It even described how and where the hands had to be placed to give the best impression. Why would any so-called professional want to burden interviewees with such silliness? Stay focused on selling your product.

As for body language, there are a few basics to follow. Sit up straight, don't slouch or lean to one side. You want to send the message that you're interested in the position and what they have to say. Pay attention and give them your undivided attention. You can lean forward, nod when you like what you hear and don't forget to smile. Have you ever had someone ask you what was wrong when there wasn't anything wrong? Apparently, your face was sending out a different message than you thought. I read a study that stated the average four-year-old child will smile about three hundred times per day. The average adult only eight times. So if you're happy, tell your face. Even if you're not happy, fake the smile. No one wants to hire a stick-in-the-mud or a sour puss.

Crossing the arms over your chest isn't necessarily a negative. It's when you do it that makes the difference. If you cross them immediately after you're asked a question, it may be interpreted as being defensive and that maybe they hit a sore spot. Try to control any itching because some people may interpret that as being nervous and unsure of your answers.

"Is there anything wrong with wearing perfume?" Not if you're going out on a date. Many people are allergic to scents and you can't take the chance that the interviewer isn't one of them. Make sure you shower and wear deodorant. That will be good enough. It's difficult to leave them with a good impression of you, if they are choking on your perfume or cologne.

"Should I show interest in their personal objects like trophies or pictures?" On the surface, this could seem like a good idea. The flaw to it is you don't know if the items belong to the interviewer or not. Quite often the ploy comes across as a transparent attempt to score points with the interviewer. An interviewee thought he would be clever and comment on the obvious photography skills of the employer. When the employer asked if the interviewee was into photography too, the interviewer had to admit he wasn't. The poor fellow couldn't tell the difference between a Pentax and a Pentium. All he accomplished was reinforcing that he didn't have much in common with the employer. Not a bright move. Don't open a conversation that you can't take part in intelligently. Remember why you're there and build the connection between you and the position.

"How do I handle interruptions and distractions?" Try to keep focused on selling your benefits but if you know that they are not listening, ask for a better time. There is little use in investing your interview time if, mentally, they are not in the room with you. They won't remember you or anything you said two minutes after you're out the door. Sympathize with them that you can see they are very busy and ask if it would be to their advantage to set up a different time to discuss your qualifications. If the interviewer was putting on a show for you to test how you would handle the situation, they are likely to decline the offer and get down to the business of interviewing. If they are up to their ass in alligators, they will appreciate your concern and flexibility. You have nothing to lose by suggesting it if they aren't focused on you anyway.

"What if I'm having a bad day?" That is the battle cry of the Bottom Feeder. They let the events of the day determine how they will approach the rest of the day. A Shark has the ability to shut the rest of the day out and focus on the moment. I don't care what has gone wrong for you that day. All you have to do is be in the zone, be on top of your game or be up and positive for the length of the interview. You can always schedule time to come unglued later but don't blow any opportunity to sell your product. Life is full of obstacles. How you deal with them will determine if you're a Shark or a Bottom Feeder.

"What if I don't understand the question?" Have you ever asked someone a question and they babbled on about something totally unrelated? It was because they didn't understand the question. Do you want to look as stupid as they did? Every question is an opportunity to sell your product. If you're unsure about what they're looking for, then ask for clarification. Asking them to clarify lets them know that you're assertive and that clear communication is important to you.

Turn off all electronic devices. Interviewers have had young people who said they could listen to both the interviewer and their disc player. I took part in an interview where my associate and I were interviewing a young woman for one of the long-term programs we were running. My associate was obviously more lenient than I was because he didn't eliminate her as a candidate until after she interrupted the interview to take the second call from her friends on her cell phone. I'm not sure if she thought she would impress us with how popular she was, but I can tell you it did not work. Shut off the phone or better yet, don't bring it to the interview.

Larry Arrance

Chapter 22. Hiring a Professional Hunter

"I heard a great deal about using a headhunter to find employment. What should I know about them?" Well there are two basic types of headhunters or what some people call recruiters. First, we have retained headhunting firms that are hired by employers to fill a specific position. They may be paid anywhere from 20 – 40% of that positions' yearly salary as a retainer. They keep the money whether or not they actually find the right candidate. Obviously, they deal in the "cream of the crop" employee. The headhunters from these firms do not advertise job openings. Most of their clientele are sought out because of their reputation for excellent work. In other words, their clients are already working and are not actively seeking new opportunities. These recruiters will sweet talk you into jumping ship and signing with their client.

Contingency headhunters cater to finding jobs for junior and mid-level positions. The company only pays them if they hire their candidate. Whether or not a retainer or contingency firm fills the position, it is the employer who picks up the tab, not you. Some firms will charge you a fee. This does not necessarily make them better. Try the no-charge firms first before you dole out your funds. Enlisting the help of the wrong type of recruiter can be terrible waste of time. Seek out firms that specialize in your field. They will have much better contacts and will have an easier time selling your product. A specialized firm won't be as broad based but their connections will run a lot deeper into your industry.

Keep in mind that you're taking someone on to market your product when you use a recruiter. Unless you're in a different city than the recruiter you should not limit your contact with them to the telephone. You should have good working relationship. This usually means meeting them in person to see if you want to sign up with this person. The benefits of working with a good headhunter is that they should be able to help groom you for the position by crafting your cover letter, upgrading your resume and tuning you up for the interview. They can greatly improve your employment package by guiding you through the negotiation for pay, benefits and perks.

Beware of recruiting firms that are just going to blanket the marketplace with your resume. This can be disastrous to your work search. Research the headhunter and make sure you're making the best choice. How broad is the headhunter's outreach? Do they focus locally, nationally or internationally? What is their background? Do they have extensive training in interpersonal communication and sales? Their skills in this area should be exceptional.

"Okay, so I've hooked up with a recruiter, what is my responsibility?" You're now in partnership with this person. One of the biggest complaints from recruiters is that lots of applicants don't return their phone calls promptly nor send in resumes when they are asked. If the recruiter has suggestions for your resume or cover letter, are you open enough to accept it and make the changes? Remember these people market people for a living. They should have a pretty good idea of what works and what doesn't. Don't put too many restrictions on your headhunter. If you will only work in a small geographical area, you might want to consider doing the job search yourself.

There are other types of recruiters out there that will be more than willing to help you find a position, which leads me to the next subject.

"Is the military a good employment opportunity?" People join the military for lots of reasons. If you're considering them as a source or employment or a possible steppingstone to further your career, make sure you do your homework. The first person you will be talking to is their recruiter. Most recruiters are honest but remember that they have quotas fill and they need you to fill that quota. So the following is a list of questions you will need to ask that recruiter. The list comes from the militarys' own web site.

1. **Get it in writing**. There is no such thing as a verbal promise. Remember **you're** signing up; so make sure you're getting the things you were promised, in writing. If you don't and you try to go after the military to come through with the missing benefits, it will be your word against the recruiter's. Who do you think will win that case?

2. **Don't make emotional decisions**. You can get caught up in the hype and patriotism of the opportunity of joining the service. Don't make your decision based on one or two visits. Take your time. This is potentially a big decision. Remember this job could take you into very dangerous situation.

3. **Go with a buddy**. You're less likely to be overwhelmed or manipulated by a well-trained, professional salesperson like a recruiter. Consider taking a friend or even better, your parents. Don't be surprised if you take a friend and he or she ends up joining because they will try to recruit them too.

4. **Can I have the job I want**? Theoretically you can. If you score high enough on the entrance test (Armed Service Vocational Aptitude Battery), you can get the job you want. It's recommended that you practice and take the test several times until you get the score you want. DO NOT enlist until you get the score you want. Make sure you know the minimum score on the test for the job you're after. If you think you can work your way up to the position, you will be in for a rude awakening. Make sure you go over the entire career path for your chosen field and what steps you will have to take to reach the destination you want.

5. **Can I be stationed where I want**? News flash! Military people move - and move often. Often if you're highly qualified, the recruiter can utilize programs that have candidates

starting at the base or in the region of their choice.

6. **Can I get paid more**? If you have qualifications that are in high demand, you could qualify for a higher rank and pay than other new recruits. But be realistic, there is a trade off for this opportunity and often the trade off is lower pay than you may get for a similar job in the marketplace. Make sure you mention any previous training like ROTC experience. This can place you above your peers. Although the base pay and veteran benefits are the same across services, opportunities for travel, job availability and promotion rates can vary greatly.

7. **Can I choose when I start**? Sometimes you can delay the intake until you finish high school or possibly avoid starting during extreme seasons like winter and summer. Also, understand that there is a difference in the length of basic training for each service. Take that into consideration.

8. **How long should I sign up for?** Naturally, you will get better benefits with a longer commitment. They are getting more out of their investment when you stay longer. The shortest term possible is two years and, if you're after specialized training or opportunities, it will likely be longer. They will offer you lots of incentives to re-enlist.

9. **Correct the contract before signing**. Hopefully, the word contract will make you realize that this isn't like trying on a pair of

pants. You can't just walk away from your commitment, should you change your mind. So take this seriously. Go over the document closely. Typos and spelling errors could hurt you in many ways. Less pay and incorrect job assignments are just a couple of the complications. Do not believe anyone who says it can be corrected later!

10. **Remember, you're signing up to be a soldier, airman, sailor, marine or coastguardsman.** Yes, you will receive the training you wanted and you may get the job you wanted but your first priority in their eyes is to serve your country. So, if you don't want to serve in the military, don't use this as your vehicle to earn money for college or casual employment. If you're not sure this is right for you, then consider joining the Reserves or National Guard. Your obligation is generally one weekend a month, plus two weeks of active duty a year.

Like most things in life, there is a trade off. If after you have had all your questions answered and you can live with the commitment, take advantage of the money and the experience and commit to making your time a great investment.

Chapter 23. Rinse and Repeat

Change happens to everyone. When I preach to students that they should be investing time and money into their next job while they are still working, I get bombarded with puzzled looks and protests. A typical protest is that they don't want to appear disloyal to their present employer. I look at it this way, you have a choice between being disloyal to them or to yourself. Which is your biggest concern, the success of their business or the success of your career? If both can be achieved at the same time, great! If it is a choice between them and you, you'd better pick you every time.

If the employer had to choose between what was good for the company and what was good for you, which would they choose? By all means, give your employer your best output and production but make sure you're protecting and promoting your career. You may move from one employer to the next but your career is going everywhere with you. You need to keep it tuned up so that it can take you more places.

It goes without saying, or at least it should, that you do your preparations for career moves on your own time. If you visit the Workopolis website, you will find a button on the homepage that is labeled "Boss Panic Button". When you click on it, it immediately closes the web page and opens a fictitious word document on your screen. Hopefully, it is meant to be humorous, because I would hate to think that you were utilizing your employer's time, equipment and money to search for a better position. You will find plenty of time during your off-hours to research companies, upgrade your marketing materials, and network. Being fired for not doing your job would free up your time for looking for a better job but it won't enhance your situation.

Regularly update your resume. This will keep your marketing tools current and will force you to focus on changing it to make it more powerful. Every three months take your resume out and study it for ways to improve it. The Japanese have a term for this kind of positive growth focus, Kaizen. It means constant and never ending improvement. Your product must never become stagnant. Sharks make sure they're keeping up on whatever is on the cutting edge of their industry and find ways to acquire the skill or training. Becoming comfortable and complacent with your skills, training and education, is the sign of a Bottom Feeder. Opportunities rarely come to you. When opportunity knocks, you still have to get up and answer the door.

If you're not sure what skills you should be developing, take a trip to your employment center or local newspaper. Ask to look through the archives of newspaper employment ads. Take notice of skills that have been repeatedly requested. Those are the skills that are obviously in demand. Acquire them and your product will be much more marketable. Why do you think the most powerful and successful companies have research and development departments? If they don't constantly improve their product line, they will become extinct or remain barely on the scene.

You must look at the time and money you spend on taking courses or attending seminars as an investment in your future marketability. Let's imagine that you attend a class that is 100 hours in length. You really apply yourself and by the end of the course you have a skill that will enable you to earn an extra $10 per hour. You have a full time job and work 2000 hours per year. So that means your new skill will earn you an extra $20,000 per year over and above what you were making. Typically, a skill needs to be replaced or upgraded every 3 years. So in a 3-year period that new skill earned you an extra $60,000 dollars. If we divide the original 100 hours into the $60,000 dollars, it would show us that you were getting paid $600 per hour to attend that class. Was it worth your time? Let's be more conservative and say that the new skill only earned you an extra $5 per hour. That means you were being paid $300 per hour to sit in the room, pick up book or just be involved in the work. Was it worth your time?

That is how a Shark views attending classes, lectures or conferences. A Bottom Feeder will only attend classes if they are paid for by someone else and, often, under coercion. My wife worked for a company that wanted their sales force to attend a motivation seminar with some of the top names in the industry providing training and inspiration. It was astounding to hear the whining and crying over what they called a waste of their time. Bottom Feeders, as a rule, don't get that if they are not moving forward they are actually losing ground. Constant learning is your ticket to future employment.

Just like you're the head of research and development for your product, you're also in charge of marketing and promotions. Instead of going home from work and carving deep impressions into your couch with your butt, go to situations where you can rub shoulders with people who can use someone with your types of skills. Your new hobby should be networking. One of my mentors told me his wife would often get annoyed at him because whether they were out at a party, attending a lecture or on vacation, he was networking. He said he couldn't take the chance that the person standing next to him wasn't going to offer him work or want to acquire his services. A Shark is always in motion looking and creating opportunities.

Even if you plan to stay with your current employer, you should be constantly marketing yourself to them. Keep them apprised of whatever new courses you're taking. Also, don't take it for granted that they are aware of everything you do on the job. Employers, managers and supervisors get busy with their own lives and jobs and may not realize how much you contribute. One woman told me that she made a point of bringing to her supervisor's attention, every three or four months, what projects she had worked on and her stellar attendance record. She averaged three raises for every one raise the other staff received.

Where do you want to be in 5 years, 10 years and beyond? I would be willing to bet big money that if you went out today and asked 10 of your friends or family, your answer would be a blank stare. Without knowing what direction we are headed and why we are headed there, we deserve to crash onto the shores of unemployment. If you take a look at some of the most successful companies, many of which are Japanese, they have plan that often goes a couple decades ahead. I often ask people where they will be in five years and they don't have a clue. I ask them what they are doing that weekend and they do know that. I run into them five years later and the only difference in their situation is that they now have another 250 weekends under their belts.

I remember from my days in high school, kids who already knew what they wanted to be when they were in grade eight. What a huge advantage they had over me. When I graduated, I still didn't have a clear idea of what I wanted to do for a career. When I run into them twenty years later, they had a lot more to show for their efforts than I did. It wasn't that I hadn't accomplished as much or had made as much effort as they had. The difference was that all of their efforts, energy and education took them in that one desired direction. Mine took me in a dozen different directions. Do you want your career to be compared to a guided missile or tumbleweed? Surprises are great for parties but not for careers.

I'm often asked what career to go after. First off, that should never be someone else's responsibility -

choosing your career. Bar rooms, psychiatric wards and counselor's offices are full of people who were forced or coaxed into going after a career that someone else chose for them. Do you know how long you will live? Unless your doctor has told you (in which case you shouldn't be reading this book, you should be out living your life), you don't know for sure. Decide what will give you the most fulfillment and enjoyment. Going after what is secure can be a recipe for resentment, boredom and a wasted life. Doing what is secure with a plan being of doing what you want after you retire is stupid. How do you know you will live to see retirement? What if you do but then you don't have the health to do the things you like? Will it have been worth it?

In my job, I've met with lots of clients that stay in positions because the pay was good or it was a very solid company with a good future. Quite often by the time they come to see me for help finding new employment, they have suffered in many ways. They may have to deal with injuries from doing jobs that they were not designed to do or their health has become seriously deteriorated. I have friends that worked for a major employer in our city. The money was good and the benefits excellent. Unfortunately, they seemed to be either sick or injured much of the time. It was their mind and body's way of telling them that they didn't belong there. They were creating ways to be away from jobs they didn't like and were not right for. Another young man told me that he would arrive for work Monday morning feeling great and in a good mood. By Friday afternoon, he was the most miserable person to be around. He was grouchy and ready to tear people's heads off. He found that when he became unemployed his spirits and his mood were much higher. Choosing the wrong career can be very costly.

Some employment counselors will recommend that you have more than one area you're interested in. I would agree. I had a client that had made a major career jump without doing any research. He had what I call, a King's job. He was the purchaser for a major organization. For him it was a great position with lots of power, perks and prestige. With lots of sales reps vying for his attention and willing to sweeten the deal to ensure the sale, he was in a very favorable position. Well, the day came when his wife thought it would be nice to perhaps finish off her career in our fair city which, by the way was much fairer than theirs.

He thought this was a great idea and quit his job figuring he could just pick up another purchaser's position here. WRONG! Those positions are highly coveted and are rarely available. Also, many companies were getting away from having one person with that much power and were distributing responsibilities to several managers. He stubbornly hung on to his search for another King's position for nearly two years. Needless to say, his unemployment benefits dwindled quickly and so did his savings. He finally gave up and took a job selling used building supplies. His work search during that two years would have been much more fruitful had he been willing to look at other possibilities.

Investigate other industries or alternate careers. The old saying that when one door closes another one opens, proves out over and over. Quite often, what looks like a detour is merely a delay. You can still get there by taking the scenic route. You will experience far less frustration when you're flexible. Instead of thinking particular job, think of particular sets of skills being utilized.

A key activity while preparing for your next opportunity is to develop and build your network of associates and friends. Harvey McKay, author of *Dig Your Well Before You're Thirty*, said it so well when he said "Find a friend before you need a friend." There is never a time when friends seem more scarce than when you need one and you realize you don't have any. Trying to find friends when you're in a needy frame of mind is like holding up a garlic covered cross to a vampire. You will drive people away. Join organizations related to fields you're considering and start connecting with your future associates. You will find that they will be able to help you through the transition.

Another avenue to consider is the self-employed route. You may find that the perfect boss for you is you. I highly recommend the book *Finding Your Perfect Work* by Sarah and Paul Edwards. They will guide you through a series of eye opening exercises that will determine if self-employment is your best bet. I promise, you will be amazed at what some people have turned into lucrative and rewarding self-employment opportunities.7

If it is possible, and it usually is, find yourself a mentor. If you're already on the job, look for the person who obviously knows the business well. Consider everyone. It won't necessarily be someone in management. Ask them to be a mentor. You may be surprised to find out that they are flattered and would be glad to help. If you think the person would be embarrassed by the request, then make a habit of asking them lots of questions. Be smart and tap into their wealth of knowledge and experience. If you look at some of the most successful people out there, they all had someone above them that helped them with their journey. I will always be very grateful to my mentor Ron Schlitt. He has always been a source of guidance and a great role model. Many of my successes happened because he had faith that I could handle the challenge and gave me a shove when needed.

If you can't find a mentor where you're now, then consider asking someone who is already successful in the industry that you're going into. If no one is available, then consider going after people who are not physically in your area or even someone who is dead. And by that I mean read books or listen to tapes by successful people. Many of the people who gave me guidance throughout my career, I have never met, yet their influence was immeasurable.

I was given the privilege of being a mentor to a young woman who attended one of my workshops. After being in my class for a few days, she told me she wanted to be a facilitator. I guided her with suggestions of what steps to take to open the right doors for the chance to instruct adult education classes. She followed the advice diligently. The work paid off because she eventually joined our staff as a facilitator. Her natural skills of connecting with people and performing in front of a crowd made her very successful as a facilitator. The position with us became a launching pad for a professional speaking career. She now travels throughout North America delivering professional workshops for an international career and personal development company.

I hope that this book and my advice will prove to be something you will look back on and say that I helped make a difference in your life and your career. So when you choose between being a Shark and a Bottom Feeder, be a SHARK!

About the Author

Larry Arrance is a professional facilitator, newspaper columnist, writing coach and writer of sales and marketing materials. He has developed and facilitated workshops on topics such as Power Resume Writing, Killer Cover Letters, Closing the Deal Interview Tactics, Fearless Public Speaking, Excelling in Times of Change, Building Solid Self-Esteem, and Unleash the Author Within.

Larry has facilitated workshops for over 4,000 job seekers and career changers. He has personally guided hundreds through the development of powerful marketing tools in their quest to gain employment. During his ten years as an employment coach and facilitator he has helped clients that ranged from those who were just entering the market, the long-termed unemployed, professionals making major career changes, and victims of restructuring.